PROSPER
WITH
ZERO-BASED
THINKING

Tom Monson

Prosper with Zero Based Thinking

The Art of Making Right Decisions

Zero-based thinking (ZBT) is a technique leaders draw on to make tough decisions--and to assess the decisions they've already made. Developed by author and motivational speaker Brian Tracy more than a decade ago, it asks the question, "If I were to start over again today, would I do anything different?"

Introduction

Zero-based thinking (ZBT) is a decision-making and problem-solving technique that encourages individuals to start from scratch or "zero" when evaluating a particular situation or making decisions. Instead of building upon existing assumptions, traditions, or processes, ZBT encourages a fresh perspective that questions the status quo and examines every aspect without any preconceived notions. This approach is often associated with greater innovation, efficiency, and a willingness to consider new ideas.

Here are some key principles and aspects of zero-based thinking:

Question Everything: ZBT encourages individuals to question and reevaluate every aspect of a situation or problem. This means not assuming that the current way of doing things is the best or only way.

No Preconceived Notions: ZBT asks people to leave their biases and preconceived notions at the door. It promotes open-mindedness and a willingness to explore unconventional solutions.

Resource Allocation: In a business context, ZBT is often used in budgeting and resource allocation. Instead of starting with the previous year's budget as a baseline, ZBT requires justifying every expense from scratch, ensuring that each expenditure is necessary and provides value.

Efficiency and Innovation: By challenging established practices, ZBT can lead to more efficient processes and innovative solutions. It allows organizations to identify and eliminate inefficiencies and allocate resources more effectively.

Risk Assessment: ZBT involves a thorough risk assessment for each decision. By starting from zero, it encourages a careful evaluation of the potential risks and rewards of each option.

Continuous Improvement: Zero-based thinking is not a one-time process. It encourages a culture of continuous improvement where decisions are continually reviewed and refined based on changing circumstances and new information.

Zero-based thinking is often used in business strategy, particularly in areas such as cost management and budgeting. However, it can also be applied to personal decision-making and problem-solving to encourage more creative and efficient solutions.

It's worth noting that zero-based thinking may not be suitable for all situations. In some cases, it may be more efficient to build upon existing knowledge and practices rather than starting from scratch. The choice to use zero-based thinking should depend on the specific context and goals of the decision-making process.

Should you use zero-based thinking in your life? The best answer is if you are living the life you dreamed of and have no more room for improvement, then probably not. On the other hand, if you are like most people, zero-based thinking can probably help you make better decisions to help you find the prosperity you seek.

Question Everything

ZBT's emphasis on questioning everything is about instilling a mindset of curiosity, critical thinking, and adaptability. It empowers individuals and organizations to move beyond conventional wisdom and explore new possibilities, ultimately leading to more efficient, effective, and innovative solutions to problems and challenges.

Challenging Assumptions

In the realm of decision-making, one of the cornerstones of Zero-Based Thinking (ZBT) is the art of challenging assumptions. This principle stands as a testament to the foundational shift that ZBT brings to the table, urging individuals and organizations alike to question the unquestionable. It's about breaking free from the clutches of conventional wisdom and daring to explore uncharted territory.

The Pitfall of Assumptions

Before we delve into the practicality of challenging assumptions, let's acknowledge the subtle dangers of assumptions. Over time, individuals and organizations can develop routines, practices, and processes that seem like the default mode of operation. These routines, often born out of necessity or historical precedent, can become so deeply ingrained that they're never scrutinized.

Consider a classic example in the corporate world. Imagine a company that has been using a particular marketing strategy for years because it has always worked, or so they assume. The leadership and marketing teams have grown accustomed to this approach, and it's become part of their identity. Here lies the potential pitfall – assuming that what has worked in the past will always be the best course of action.

The ZBT Approach

Now, let's bring Zero-Based Thinking into the picture. ZBT encourages individuals and organizations to pause, reflect, and challenge these long-standing assumptions. It insists on asking a simple but profoundly impactful question: "Why are we doing it this way?" This question serves as a catalyst for change, a spark of curiosity that ignites the flames of innovation.

Example

The Marketing Overhaul

Let's revisit the scenario of our marketing-savvy company. Under ZBT's influence, the marketing team decides to embark on a bold journey of challenging assumptions. Instead of blindly continuing with their time-tested strategy, they assemble a diverse team for a brainstorming session.

The team starts by dissecting their current approach, laying bare all the assumptions that underpin it. They question the assumption that their target audience will always respond favorably to the same messaging. They question the assumption that their chosen advertising channels are still the most effective. They even question the assumption that their competitors will follow the same predictable patterns.

This rigorous examination reveals something astounding – there are alternative approaches and untapped opportunities waiting to be explored. The team considers unconventional strategies, redefines their target audience, and experiments with emerging advertising platforms.

The result? A groundbreaking marketing campaign that not only captures the attention of their audience but also propels the company to the forefront of their industry. By challenging their deep-rooted assumptions, the marketing team has opened doors to innovation and success they never thought possible.

Challenging assumptions is more than a theoretical exercise; it's a practical catalyst for change and innovation. ZBT encourages individuals and organizations to step out of their comfort zones, question the status quo, and explore new possibilities. By doing so, they can uncover novel solutions, drive efficiency, and reach new heights in decision-making and problem-solving. In the journey of decision-making, ZBT invites

you to challenge assumptions and discover the untapped
potential that lies beyond the boundaries of conventionality.

Breaking Down Traditions

Traditions and established practices have long been the backbone of cultures, organizations, and even personal routines. They provide stability, a sense of continuity, and often hold deep sentimental value. However, there's a catch – traditions can sometimes become a barrier to progress and innovation. That's where Zero-Based Thinking (ZBT) steps in, urging us to break down these traditional barriers in favor of fresh, forward-thinking approaches.

The Power and Peril of Traditions

Traditions, whether they pertain to family customs, corporate rituals, or societal norms, often serve essential functions. They create a sense of identity and cohesion, providing a comforting framework within which individuals and groups operate. However, as the world evolves at an unprecedented pace, clinging to traditions without scrutiny can stifle growth and hinder adaptability.

Example:

Imagine a historic bookstore with a time-honored tradition of cataloging its extensive collection using handwritten index cards. For decades, this method served the store well, exuding a nostalgic charm that drew book enthusiasts from far and wide. The staff had become proficient in this tradition, and it was a point of pride for the store's identity.

Embracing Zero-Based Thinking: A Bookstore Reimagined

Here's where Zero-Based Thinking enters the scene. The store's management, inspired by the ZBT philosophy, decides to examine their cherished tradition with fresh eyes. They ask the pivotal question: "Is this traditional cataloging system still the most efficient and effective way to manage our inventory?"

In their pursuit of a more innovative approach, they explore digital cataloging systems, automated inventory management software, and cloud-based databases. While these options challenge the cozy familiarity of their handwritten cards, they also promise unprecedented efficiency, real-time data accessibility, and the ability to expand their customer base through online sales.

After a thorough evaluation, the store decides to transition to a state-of-the-art digital cataloging system. The transition is met with mixed emotions – some staff members are nostalgic about the old ways, while others are excited about the possibilities of the new system.

The Outcomes of Innovation

In the months that follow, the bookstore experiences a transformation. With the newfound efficiency of their digital catalog, they can respond rapidly to customer requests, provide accurate inventory data online, and offer a seamless shopping experience both in-store and on their website.

Sales soar as the store reaches a broader audience, and their reputation for innovation attracts new customers. While the handwritten index cards remain in a display case as a nod to their heritage, the bookstore has successfully embraced modernity without forsaking its tradition entirely.

The example of the bookstore illustrates the power of Zero-Based Thinking in breaking down traditions that may no longer serve their intended purpose. ZBT encourages us to assess whether our practices, no matter how cherished, are still relevant in a rapidly changing world. It's not about discarding traditions wholesale but about finding a balance between the old and the new, the sentimental and the pragmatic.

In the grand tapestry of decision-making, Zero-Based Thinking invites us to transcend the comfort of tradition and explore innovative pathways that can lead to increased efficiency, enhanced competitiveness, and continued relevance in an ever-evolving landscape. It's a call to action to break down the barriers of tradition and embrace the winds of change to reach new heights of success.

Avoiding Complacency

Complacency, often masked as comfort with the status quo, can be a silent saboteur of progress and growth. It's the state of being satisfied with current circumstances, even when they may no longer be optimal. Zero-Based Thinking (ZBT) emerges as a beacon of proactivity, challenging complacency by instilling a mindset that actively seeks improvement and innovation.

The Seductive Trap of Complacency

Complacency creeps into various aspects of life, from personal routines to corporate cultures. When individuals or organizations reach a point where they're content with the way things are, they may inadvertently close the door to innovation and growth. After all, why fix something that doesn't appear to be broken?

Example

Imagine a well-established tech company that has long dominated its niche market. They've enjoyed years of success with a product that's become synonymous with quality and reliability. Their customers are loyal, and their revenue is steady. In this seemingly comfortable scenario, complacency begins to set in.

Zero-Based Thinking Sparks Change

Now, enter Zero-Based Thinking. It's a philosophy that challenges the very essence of complacency. It demands that individuals and organizations question the status quo relentlessly. The key question here is, "Is there a better way to do this?"

Our tech company, influenced by ZBT principles, starts to scrutinize their long-standing product. They question whether it's still meeting the evolving needs of their customer base or if they're merely coasting on their reputation. This introspection is uncomfortable but essential.

The Tech Company's Pivot

In their quest to avoid complacency, the tech company decides to pivot. They recognize that emerging technologies and changing consumer preferences are shifting the landscape. Instead of resting on their laurels, they invest in research and development to create a product that not only meets current needs but anticipates future trends.

The transition is challenging, requiring them to retrain staff, adapt their supply chain, and communicate the changes to loyal customers. But the results are worth it. The company not only maintains its market dominance but expands into new markets and remains at the forefront of innovation.

The Transformative Power of Proactivity

The example of our tech company demonstrates how Zero-Based Thinking actively combats complacency. By continually evaluating the relevance and effectiveness of their practices, they avoid stagnation and seize opportunities for improvement. ZBT fosters a culture that welcomes change as a means to stay competitive and deliver better outcomes.

In the grand narrative of decision-making, Zero-Based Thinking stands as a bulwark against complacency. It's a clarion call to action, urging individuals and organizations to avoid the seductive trap of settling for the status quo. Instead, it encourages them to embrace change, seek improvement, and proactively innovate to maintain relevance and achieve lasting success.

ZBT is not just a philosophy; it's a mindset that champions the pursuit of excellence and growth, ensuring that complacency never finds a comfortable home in the hearts and minds of those who dare to think without bounds.

Exploring Alternatives

Exploring alternatives is the heartbeat of innovation and progress. In a world brimming with complexities, Zero-Based Thinking (ZBT) serves as a guiding light, beckoning us to venture beyond the realms of the obvious and challenge the ordinary. It's an approach that encourages individuals not to settle for the first solution that comes to mind but to embrace the thrill of exploring unconventional options that can lead to fresh, improved, and game-changing outcomes.

The Habit of Settling for the Familiar

It's human nature to gravitate towards what's known and familiar. When faced with a problem or decision, the mind often defaults to the tried-and-true, the solutions that have worked in the past. While this tendency is not without merit, it can inadvertently limit our capacity for innovation and growth.

Example

Imagine a seasoned chef in a renowned restaurant known for its classic dishes. Customers flock to the restaurant for its signature menu items, and the chef has honed these recipes to perfection over the years. However, as time goes by, the chef notices a decline in customer engagement and excitement.

Zero-Based Thinking Sparks the Journey

This is where Zero-Based Thinking makes its entrance. It demands that we step out of our comfort zones and challenge the notion that the existing path is the only path. It encourages us to ask, "Are there alternative ways to achieve the same or even better results?"

In our restaurant scenario, the chef, influenced by ZBT principles, decides to embark on a culinary exploration. They assemble a team of chefs, each with diverse culinary backgrounds, and they initiate brainstorming sessions. The mission? To reimagine the restaurant's menu while preserving the essence of what customers love.

The Culinary Revolution

Under the banner of ZBT, the restaurant undergoes a transformation. Instead of resting on the laurels of their signature dishes, they introduce a rotating menu that features innovative fusion cuisine. The once-static atmosphere now buzzes with anticipation as customers look forward to discovering new, unexpected flavors.

While not every experiment is an immediate success, the restaurant's willingness to explore alternatives pays off in the long run. They attract a new clientele seeking unique dining experiences, and their reputation as a culinary trendsetter soars.

The Art of Discovery Through Exploration

This example underscores how ZBT empowers individuals and organizations to explore alternatives beyond the conventional. It's about embracing the thrill of discovery, even in the face of uncertainty. Through the lens of ZBT, settling for the familiar is not an option, and stagnation becomes the enemy of progress.

In the grand tapestry of decision-making, Zero-Based Thinking invites us to be intrepid explorers of alternatives. It reminds us that there is no monopoly on innovation, and the uncharted paths often lead to the most remarkable destinations. ZBT is a call to action, urging us to question everything and uncover new, potentially superior solutions that can revolutionize our lives, our businesses, and our world. It is a testament to the power of exploration, the thrill of discovery, and the boundless potential of human ingenuity.

Adapting to Change

Change is the only constant in today's dynamic world. As new technologies emerge, markets evolve, and societal shifts occur, individuals and organizations must adapt to remain relevant and successful. Zero-Based Thinking (ZBT) is a guiding philosophy that recognizes the paramount importance of adaptability and encourages individuals to embrace change by regularly reassessing their strategies and approaches. In a rapidly evolving landscape, ZBT is the compass that points us towards the path of continuous adaptation.

The Challenge of Stagnation

Stagnation is the adversary of progress. When individuals or organizations become complacent and adhere rigidly to strategies that once yielded success, they risk falling behind the curve. What worked well in the past may no longer be suitable in a world where the ground is constantly shifting beneath our feet.

Example

Imagine a once-thriving brick-and-mortar retailer that built its empire on the traditional in-store shopping experience. For years, they enjoyed steady foot traffic and loyal customers. However, the rise of e-commerce has begun to chip away at their market share, and they are now faced with a critical decision: adapt or face irrelevance.

Zero-Based Thinking and the Call to Adapt

Enter Zero-Based Thinking. It serves as a wake-up call, urging individuals and organizations to confront the winds of change head-on. ZBT invites us to regularly evaluate our strategies and ask the essential question: "Is our current approach still the most effective way to achieve our goals?"

In the case of our brick-and-mortar retailer, they decide to apply ZBT principles to navigate the shifting retail landscape. They explore innovative ways to integrate e-commerce into their business model, including launching a user-friendly website and leveraging data analytics to enhance customer experiences.

A Retailer's Transformation

As a result of their ZBT-inspired adaptation, the retailer experiences a transformation. They not only survive the e-commerce onslaught but thrive in the new retail landscape. By combining the strengths of both online and in-store shopping, they create a seamless omnichannel experience that attracts a broader customer base.

Their adaptability pays off in other ways too. They respond swiftly to changing customer preferences and market trends, introducing new product lines and personalized shopping recommendations. In doing so, they not only regain market share but also become a retail innovator, setting the standard for others in the industry.

The Power of Continuous Adaptation

The example of the retailer illustrates the transformative power of ZBT's emphasis on adaptability. By regularly reassessing their strategies and embracing change, they not only survive but thrive in a rapidly evolving market.

In the grand narrative of decision-making, Zero-Based Thinking stands as a guardian of adaptability. It is a steadfast reminder that in a world marked by change, stagnation is not an option. ZBT empowers individuals and organizations to evolve with the times, to reevaluate their strategies, and to navigate the complex terrain of a dynamic world.

ZBT embodies the spirit of continuous adaptation, enabling us to not only weather the storms of change but to harness their energy to sail towards new horizons of opportunity and growth. It is the beacon that lights our way as we navigate the ever-shifting seas of progress and innovation.

Encouraging Continuous Learning

In an era defined by rapid technological advancements and ever-evolving knowledge, the journey of learning never truly ends. Zero-Based Thinking (ZBT) recognizes that perpetual curiosity and the pursuit of improvement are the cornerstones of success. It advocates for a culture that not only questions everything but also fosters continuous learning, ensuring that individuals and organizations remain agile and informed in a rapidly changing world.

The Challenge of Stagnation in Knowledge

Stagnation in knowledge can be as perilous as stagnation in any other aspect of life. When individuals or organizations cease to expand their horizons and question their existing beliefs and practices, they risk becoming obsolete in a world where information and innovation flow ceaselessly.

Example

Imagine a seasoned professional in the field of marketing who has relied on traditional advertising methods throughout their career. They've achieved success using these methods, and their reputation is well-established. However, the landscape of marketing is undergoing a paradigm shift with the rise of digital and social media platforms. Our professional faces a choice: adapt to the new landscape or risk becoming irrelevant.

Zero-Based Thinking: The Catalyst for Continuous Learning

This is where Zero-Based Thinking steps in. It urges us not only to question everything but also to continually ask, "What else can we learn, and how can we improve?" ZBT champions the idea that learning is an ongoing journey, not a destination. It encourages individuals and organizations to remain inquisitive, stay informed about emerging trends and technologies, and be open to incorporating new knowledge into their decision-making processes.

The Marketer's Evolution

Inspired by ZBT principles, our marketing professional embarks on a journey of continuous learning. They enroll in courses on digital marketing, immerse themselves in social media trends, and engage with thought leaders in the field. They also encourage their team to do the same, fostering a culture of perpetual growth within their organization.

As a result, our marketer not only adapts to the changing marketing landscape but becomes a trailblazer in leveraging digital platforms for advertising. They pioneer innovative campaigns that resonate with modern consumers, proving that continuous learning is the key to staying at the forefront of the industry.

The Power of Lifelong Learning

This example demonstrates the transformative power of ZBT's commitment to continuous learning. In a world where knowledge doubles at an astonishing rate, ZBT is the guiding force that ensures individuals and organizations remain not just relevant but pioneering in their fields.

In the grand scheme of decision-making, Zero-Based Thinking serves as the conductor of continuous learning. It is a symphony that celebrates the curiosity to question, the hunger for knowledge, and the commitment to improvement. ZBT propels us forward, reminding us that in a world defined by constant change, the pursuit of knowledge is an eternal melody that leads to enduring success and innovation. It is the anthem of those who choose to question everything and embrace the transformative power of lifelong learning.

Fostering Innovation

Innovation, the lifeblood of progress, thrives when individuals and organizations dare to challenge the status quo and think creatively. Zero-Based Thinking (ZBT) is a structured approach that acts as a beacon for innovation. It understands that questioning established norms is the birthplace of groundbreaking ideas and provides the fertile ground where innovation flourishes.

The Innovation Conundrum

Innovation is not a linear process; it often emerges from unconventional thinking and the courage to depart from the beaten path. However, within many organizations and individuals, the fear of failure or the comfort of the familiar can stifle creative thought, leading to a stagnation of innovative ideas.

Example

Consider a tech company that has long relied on a traditional hierarchical structure. Although it has enjoyed success in the past, it now finds itself grappling with the need for more agile and innovative approaches to remain competitive in the fast-paced tech industry. The challenge is to foster innovation in an environment accustomed to established hierarchies and processes.

Zero-Based Thinking: The Spark of Innovation

Enter Zero-Based Thinking. ZBT challenges this tech company to question the hierarchical norms and entrenched practices. It prompts them to ask, "Is there a better way to encourage innovation and adaptability?" This inquiry becomes the catalyst for transformative change.

The company decides to implement a ZBT-inspired innovation program. They encourage employees at all levels to share their ideas without fear of judgment. They break down traditional hierarchies, creating cross-functional teams that collaborate on projects. The result is a surge of creativity and innovation that was previously stifled.

Example: The Innovation Revolution

As a result of ZBT-inspired changes, our tech company undergoes an innovation revolution. Employees, once hesitant to speak up, now freely share their ideas and collaborate across departments. The company hosts hackathons and innovation challenges, where employees are encouraged to think outside the box.

One such challenge results in the development of a revolutionary product that disrupts the market. This product, born from the company's newfound culture of innovation, propels them to the forefront of the industry, leaving their competitors in awe.

The Creative Renaissance

This example illustrates how ZBT can serve as a creative renaissance. By challenging the status quo and encouraging innovative thinking, it fosters an environment where new ideas flourish. It is the bridge between tradition and progress, the roadmap to unlocking innovation's boundless potential.

In the symphony of decision-making, Zero-Based Thinking stands as a conductor of innovation. It is the melody that inspires individuals and organizations to question, to dream, and to pioneer. ZBT empowers us to challenge established norms and break free from the constraints of convention, ultimately leading us to the threshold of innovation's limitless realm. It is the anthem of those who choose to question everything and, in doing so, ignite the fires of innovation that illuminate our world.

Preconceived Notions

Zero-Based Thinking's emphasis on avoiding preconceived notions is about promoting open-mindedness, objectivity, and adaptability. It enables individuals and organizations to break free from mental constraints, explore unconventional solutions, and foster a culture of innovation and continuous improvement. This approach ultimately leads to more effective and forward-thinking decision-making processes.

Open-Mindedness

Open-mindedness is a mindset characterized by a willingness to explore, learn, and adapt in the face of new information or alternative viewpoints. In the context of ZBT, open-mindedness plays a pivotal role in challenging the status quo and driving innovation. Here are some key aspects to consider:

Receptivity to New Ideas: Open-minded individuals are receptive to ideas that may challenge their existing beliefs or methods. They are not bound by tradition or preconceived notions and are open to exploring innovative solutions, even if they initially appear unconventional.

Critical Thinking: Open-mindedness is closely tied to critical thinking. It involves the ability to objectively evaluate information, evidence, and arguments without undue bias. This critical approach allows individuals to make informed decisions based on rational analysis rather than emotional attachment to existing ideas.

Diverse Perspectives: Open-mindedness thrives on exposure to diverse perspectives and viewpoints. It encourages individuals to seek out different voices, backgrounds, and experiences to gain a broader understanding of a problem or decision. Diverse perspectives often lead to more robust and creative solutions.

Adaptability: Open-minded individuals are adaptable. They are willing to adjust their strategies or approaches when presented with compelling evidence or data that suggests a more effective path. This adaptability is essential in fast-changing environments.

Conflict Resolution: Open-mindedness is instrumental in resolving conflicts constructively. When conflicts arise, open-minded individuals are more likely to engage in productive dialogue, find common ground, and arrive at mutually beneficial solutions.

Continuous Learning: Open-mindedness is intertwined with a commitment to lifelong learning. Those who maintain open minds are continually seeking opportunities to expand their knowledge and skills, staying updated on emerging trends and best practices.

Example:

Let's consider an example of open-mindedness in the business world:

A technology company has been using a specific software development methodology for years, and it has been generally successful. However, as the industry evolves, they notice that competitors are gaining a competitive edge by adopting a new and unconventional development approach known as "agile development." Initially, some team members are resistant to change, as they are comfortable with their existing methodology.

In this scenario, a leader within the company embraces open-mindedness. They encourage team members to attend seminars, training sessions, and conferences on agile development. They also invite experts from other industries to share their experiences with agile practices. Through this exposure to diverse perspectives and new information, team members begin to see the potential benefits of agile development, including faster product delivery, increased customer satisfaction, and adaptability to changing market demands.

As a result, the company decides to transition to agile development, a move that ultimately enhances their competitiveness and product quality. The open-mindedness of the leader and the team members allowed them to consider an unconventional approach and adapt to the evolving industry landscape, leading to innovation and growth.

In essence, open-mindedness, when integrated into decision-making processes, encourages exploration, flexibility, and a readiness to embrace change, all of which are essential elements of successful problem-solving and innovation.

Avoiding Confirmation Bias

Confirmation bias is a cognitive bias that can hinder rational decision-making and problem-solving. It occurs when individuals selectively seek, interpret, and remember information that aligns with their existing beliefs, while disregarding or downplaying information that contradicts those beliefs. ZBT recognizes the importance of overcoming confirmation bias and actively encourages individuals to adopt a more open and objective mindset. Here are key aspects to consider:

Awareness of Bias: ZBT begins with the awareness that confirmation bias is a common cognitive tendency. Acknowledging this bias is the first step in mitigating its impact on decision-making.

Information Exploration: ZBT prompts individuals to actively seek out a diverse range of information sources and viewpoints. This includes considering data, opinions, and perspectives that challenge their existing beliefs. By doing so, individuals gain a more comprehensive understanding of a problem or decision.

Critical Evaluation: ZBT encourages individuals to critically evaluate the credibility and validity of information, regardless of whether it confirms or contradicts their beliefs. This involves assessing the source of the information, the quality of evidence, and the methodology used to gather data.

Constructive Disagreement: ZBT fosters an environment where constructive disagreement is welcomed. Individuals are encouraged to engage in discussions with colleagues, peers, or experts who hold different perspectives. These discussions can lead to a more well-rounded analysis of the issue at hand.

Continuous Learning: ZBT aligns with the idea of continuous learning. Individuals are motivated to challenge their own assumptions and update their beliefs based on new evidence or information. This adaptability leads to more informed decision-making over time.

Example

Let's consider an example of avoiding confirmation bias in a corporate decision-making context:

A company is considering whether to invest in a new product development project. The project manager, who is enthusiastic about the idea, conducts initial market research and gathers data that seem to support the project's potential success. The manager presents this data to the executive team, emphasizing the positive aspects of the project.

In this scenario, ZBT principles come into play when the executive team recognizes the potential for confirmation bias. To counteract this bias, they take several actions:

Diverse Data Sources: The executive team actively seeks data and market research from multiple sources, including independent third-party research firms and industry experts, to gain a more comprehensive view of the market landscape.

Critical Evaluation: They critically evaluate the quality of the data presented by the project manager. This involves examining the methodology, sample size, and potential biases in the data collection process.

Soliciting Contrary Opinions: The executive team invites dissenting opinions and challenges the assumptions underlying the project. They encourage team members to voice concerns and explore potential risks and drawbacks.

Scenario Analysis: ZBT prompts the team to conduct scenario analysis, including assessing the potential consequences of both project success and failure. This allows for a more balanced consideration of the decision's implications.

Iterative Decision-Making: Instead of making a hasty decision based solely on initial data, the executive team engages in iterative decision-making. They continuously review and update their assessment as new information becomes available, allowing for a more informed and objective final decision.

By actively avoiding confirmation bias and embracing the principles of ZBT, the executive team ensures a more well-rounded evaluation of the new product development project. This approach enhances the likelihood of making a decision that is grounded in objective analysis rather than preexisting beliefs, ultimately leading to more effective and informed choices in the corporate environment.

Diversity of Thought

Diversity of thought refers to the inclusion of a wide range of perspectives, viewpoints, and ideas within a team or organization. ZBT recognizes that fostering diversity of thought is essential for robust problem-solving and decision-making. It encourages individuals to challenge their preconceived notions and actively seek out unconventional ideas. Here are key aspects to consider:

Cultivating an Inclusive Environment: ZBT promotes an inclusive and open environment where all team members feel comfortable sharing their unique perspectives, regardless of their background or position. This inclusivity encourages the free exchange of ideas.

Questioning Assumptions: ZBT starts with the premise that assumptions can limit creativity and innovation. It encourages individuals to question their own and others' assumptions and consider alternative viewpoints.

Challenging the Status Quo: ZBT prompts individuals to challenge the status quo and avoid clinging to traditional or well-established practices solely because they are familiar. It creates a culture where continuous improvement and innovation are valued.

Fostering Creativity: Diversity of thought is a catalyst for creativity. ZBT encourages the exploration of unconventional and novel ideas, which can lead to innovative solutions to complex problems.

Problem-Solving: When teams embrace diversity of thought, they are better equipped to tackle complex problems. Different perspectives can lead to a more comprehensive understanding of the problem and a wider range of potential solutions.

Example

Let's consider an example of diversity of thought within a product design team:

A tech company is developing a new smartphone, and the product design team is tasked with creating a user-friendly interface. Traditionally, the team members have always followed industry-standard design principles, which have yielded successful products in the past.

However, in line with ZBT principles, the team decides to encourage diversity of thought in the design process:

Cross-Functional Collaboration: The design team invites members from different departments, including software developers, marketers, and customer support, to join the design brainstorming sessions. This brings together a diverse set of skills, perspectives, and experiences.

Incorporating User Feedback: ZBT emphasizes the importance of user feedback. The team actively seeks input from a wide range of users, including those with varying levels of tech-savviness, age groups, and cultural backgrounds. This feedback challenges their assumptions about user preferences.

Unconventional Ideas: During the design process, team members are encouraged to propose unconventional ideas, even if they deviate from established design norms. This includes exploring new navigation patterns, user interface elements, and accessibility features.

Prototype Iteration: The team creates multiple prototypes based on different design concepts and gathers feedback from a diverse group of testers. This iterative process allows them to refine the design based on real-world user experiences.

Data-Driven Decision-Making: ZBT encourages the team to rely on data and usability testing results rather than personal biases. They analyze user interaction data to identify areas where the design can be improved.

As a result of embracing diversity of thought and ZBT principles, the product design team develops a smartphone interface that is not only user-friendly but also innovative and adaptable to a broader range of user needs and preferences. The diversity of perspectives within the team and the willingness to challenge assumptions contribute to the creation of a product that stands out in the market and resonates with a wider audience.

Exploring Unconventional Solutions

Exploring unconventional solutions is about breaking away from traditional or expected ways of thinking and problem-solving. ZBT recognizes that innovation often arises from considering ideas and approaches that challenge established norms. Here are key aspects to consider:

Thinking Outside the Box: ZBT encourages individuals to think beyond the confines of conventional or "inside the box" solutions. It promotes creativity by asking, "What if we did things differently?"

Embracing Risk: Unconventional solutions can involve taking calculated risks. ZBT acknowledges that not all unconventional ideas will succeed, but it encourages a willingness to experiment and learn from failures.

Cross-Disciplinary Insights: ZBT promotes seeking inspiration and insights from unrelated fields or industries. Sometimes, unconventional solutions emerge when concepts from one domain are applied to another.

Diverse Perspectives: Encouraging diversity of thought, as mentioned earlier, can lead to unconventional solutions. Different backgrounds and viewpoints can inspire fresh approaches to problems.

Iterative Experimentation: ZBT often involves iterative experimentation, where unconventional ideas are tested, refined, and retested. This allows for the development of innovative solutions over time.

Example

Let's consider an example of exploring unconventional solutions in the context of the automotive industry:

A car manufacturer is facing a challenge in improving fuel efficiency for its vehicles, a key factor for both environmental sustainability and cost savings. Traditionally, the company has relied on incremental improvements to engine technology and aerodynamics to achieve better fuel economy.

However, embracing ZBT principles, the manufacturer decides to explore unconventional solutions:

Alternative Fuels: Instead of focusing solely on improving gasoline or diesel engines, the company explores alternative fuels, such as hydrogen fuel cells, electric powertrains, or even hybrid solutions. These unconventional fuel sources have the potential to significantly increase fuel efficiency and reduce emissions.

Lightweight Materials: The company considers unconventional materials like carbon fiber composites, aluminum alloys, or advanced polymers to reduce vehicle weight. Lighter vehicles require less energy to operate, leading to improved fuel efficiency.

Collaboration with Tech Companies: Recognizing the increasing role of technology in automotive innovation, the manufacturer explores partnerships with tech companies to integrate cutting-edge software and sensors that optimize engine performance and driving habits.

Vehicle Redesign: Instead of adhering to traditional vehicle designs, the manufacturer explores radical redesigns that reduce air resistance and improve aerodynamics. This might include innovative vehicle shapes or even changes in seating arrangements.

Energy Recovery Systems: The company explores unconventional ways to recover and reuse energy, such as regenerative braking systems or solar panels integrated into the vehicle's body.

[38]

Behavioral Change: ZBT also considers unconventional solutions related to driver behavior. The company might invest in technologies that provide real-time feedback to encourage more fuel-efficient driving habits.

Over time, the manufacturer's commitment to exploring unconventional solutions leads to the development of a hybrid vehicle that combines hydrogen fuel cells with regenerative braking technology. This innovative solution not only achieves exceptional fuel efficiency but also significantly reduces emissions. It becomes a competitive advantage in the market and positions the manufacturer as a leader in environmentally conscious transportation.

In this example, Zero-Based Thinking's emphasis on exploring unconventional solutions allows the car manufacturer to break free from traditional constraints and discover a game-changing innovation in the automotive industry. This illustrates how challenging preconceived notions and thinking creatively can lead to breakthroughs and competitive advantages.

Learning from Failure

Learning from failure is a critical aspect of personal and organizational growth. ZBT recognizes that preconceived notions can often hinder the ability to learn from failures by attributing them to external factors or reinforcing existing beliefs. Here are key aspects to consider:

Accountability: ZBT encourages individuals to take ownership of their failures rather than placing blame on external factors. This accountability mindset fosters a sense of responsibility for one's actions and decisions.

Objective Analysis: Instead of reacting emotionally to failure, ZBT promotes objective analysis. It encourages individuals to examine the root causes of failure, identify areas for improvement, and consider alternative approaches.

Continuous Improvement: Learning from failure is synonymous with a commitment to continuous improvement. ZBT emphasizes the importance of applying the lessons learned to refine future decisions and actions.

Resilience: ZBT recognizes that setbacks and failures are part of any journey toward success. It encourages resilience by viewing failure as an opportunity for growth rather than a defeat.

Innovation: Sometimes, failures can lead to innovative solutions. ZBT encourages individuals to explore unconventional ideas and approaches that may arise from analyzing past failures.

Example

Let's consider an example of learning from failure in the context of a tech startup:

A tech startup is developing a new mobile app that aims to revolutionize the way people organize and manage their tasks. The initial launch of the app receives a lukewarm response from users, and the download numbers are far below the company's expectations. Traditional thinking might lead to blaming external factors or assuming that the market is not ready for such an app.

However, embracing ZBT principles, the startup takes a different approach to learning from failure:

Objective Analysis: Instead of making assumptions, the startup conducts a detailed analysis of user feedback and usage data. They discover that users find the app's user interface confusing, and certain key features are not functioning as expected.

User-Centered Redesign: Rather than giving up on the app, the startup decides to embark on a user-centered redesign process. They involve users in the design process, seeking their input and preferences to improve the app's usability.

Iterative Development: ZBT encourages the startup to take an iterative approach. They release updated versions of the app with improvements based on user feedback, continually refining and enhancing the user experience.

Market Research: The company also conducts in-depth market research to understand users' needs and preferences better. They discover that there is a demand for certain unique features that were not initially considered.

Pivot and Innovation: In the process of learning from failure, the startup pivots its strategy. They integrate the unique features identified through market research, differentiating their app from competitors. This innovative approach captures the attention of a niche audience.

As a result of embracing ZBT principles and learning from their initial failure, the tech startup successfully relaunches its app with a user-friendly design and unique features. User engagement and download numbers increase significantly, and the app gains traction in the market. What seemed like a failure initially becomes a valuable learning experience that leads to innovation and ultimately, success.

This example illustrates how ZBT encourages individuals and organizations to view failure as an opportunity for growth, innovation, and improvement rather than a setback. It emphasizes the importance of objective analysis and a commitment to learning and adaptation in the face of setbacks.

Adaptability

Adaptability is the ability to adjust to new conditions, circumstances, or information. ZBT recognizes that clinging to preconceived notions can hinder adaptability, especially in a rapidly changing world. Here are key aspects to consider:

Embracing Change: ZBT encourages individuals and organizations to embrace change rather than resist it. It acknowledges that change is a constant in today's world and that adaptability is a valuable skill.

Open-Mindedness: An open-minded approach, as promoted by ZBT, is closely tied to adaptability. It involves being receptive to new ideas, information, and perspectives, even if they challenge existing beliefs.

Flexibility: Adaptability requires flexibility in thinking and action. ZBT encourages individuals to be flexible in their approaches and strategies, willing to pivot or adjust when circumstances change.

Proactive Problem-Solving: ZBT promotes proactive problem-solving in the face of challenges. Instead of becoming stuck in old ways of thinking, individuals are encouraged to seek innovative solutions when confronted with obstacles.

Continuous Learning: Adaptability is intertwined with a commitment to continuous learning and improvement. ZBT encourages individuals and organizations to stay updated on emerging trends, technologies, and best practices.

Example

Let's consider an example of adaptability in the context of a small business facing market changes:

A small, family-owned bakery has been operating successfully for several decades, using traditional recipes and marketing strategies. However, in recent years, they have noticed a decline in customer traffic and sales due to changing consumer preferences and increased competition from larger bakeries and online ordering platforms.

Embracing ZBT principles, the bakery takes steps to adapt to the changing landscape:

Market Research: The bakery conducts thorough market research to understand the evolving preferences of customers. They discover that consumers are increasingly looking for healthier and gluten-free options.

Product Diversification: Based on the research, the bakery adapts its product offerings to include healthier and gluten-free baked goods. They also experiment with new flavor combinations and seasonal specialties.

Digital Presence: Recognizing the importance of an online presence, the bakery invests in a user-friendly website and online ordering system. They also engage with customers through social media to promote their new products and special promotions.

Training and Skill Development: ZBT encourages the bakery to invest in staff training to learn new recipes and baking techniques required for the updated product line.

Customer Feedback: The bakery actively seeks customer feedback on the new products and services. They use this feedback to make ongoing adjustments and improvements.

As a result of these adaptability efforts, the bakery successfully repositions itself in the market. They attract a new customer base interested in healthier options, and their online presence brings in additional revenue. While the traditional recipes and practices still have their place, the bakery's adaptability to changing customer preferences ensures its continued success in a competitive market.

This example demonstrates how ZBT's emphasis on adaptability encourages businesses and individuals to remain open to change, innovate, and adjust their strategies to meet evolving circumstances. By doing so, they can thrive in an ever-changing world.

Fostering a Culture of Innovation

Fostering a culture of innovation is a critical outcome of Zero-Based Thinking (ZBT) that encourages organizations to challenge preconceived notions and think creatively. Such a culture promotes continuous improvement, adaptability, and the exploration of new ideas. Here are key aspects to consider:

Openness to New Ideas: ZBT encourages teams to explore unconventional and innovative solutions rather than relying on existing knowledge or practices. This openness to new ideas is essential for fostering innovation.

Risk-Taking: A culture of innovation often goes hand-in-hand with a willingness to take calculated risks. ZBT's approach of questioning everything can lead to more calculated risk-taking as teams seek innovative solutions.

Collaboration: Innovation often thrives in collaborative environments. ZBT promotes open communication and cross-functional collaboration, enabling different perspectives to contribute to the development of innovative solutions.

Continuous Learning: Cultures of innovation prioritize continuous learning and adaptation. ZBT encourages employees to learn from both successes and failures, promoting a growth mindset.

Resource Allocation for Innovation: ZBT allows organizations to allocate resources strategically, directing investments toward innovative projects and initiatives that have the potential to drive growth and competitive advantage.

Example

Let's consider how ZBT fosters a culture of innovation within a technology company:

A technology company is known for its innovative software products but wants to further cultivate a culture of innovation. They adopt ZBT principles as part of their strategic approach:

Challenging Assumptions: The company encourages employees at all levels to challenge assumptions and question why things are done a certain way. For example, they question whether there's a better way to design user interfaces or streamline development processes.

Innovation Workshops: The company holds regular innovation workshops where cross-functional teams come together to brainstorm and propose innovative ideas. These sessions are facilitated to ensure that preconceived notions are set aside, allowing fresh ideas to emerge.

Innovation Awards: To recognize and reward innovative thinking, the company introduces an annual innovation award program. Employees are encouraged to submit their innovative ideas, and winning ideas receive resources and support to be developed into products or processes.

Resource Allocation: ZBT helps the company allocate resources to support innovative projects. They ensure that innovative initiatives receive the necessary funding and talent to bring them to fruition.

Learning from Failure: The company embraces a culture where failure is seen as a stepping stone to success. Teams are encouraged to analyze failures objectively, extract lessons, and apply them to future projects.

Leadership Support: The leadership team actively supports and participates in innovation initiatives, setting an example for the entire organization.

Over time, the technology company experiences several benefits from fostering a culture of innovation through ZBT:

The company generates a steady stream of innovative product ideas.

Employees feel empowered to contribute creative solutions and take ownership of their projects.

Successful innovations lead to competitive advantages in the market.

A culture of innovation becomes a key differentiator in attracting top talent.

The company remains agile and adaptable in a rapidly changing industry.

This example illustrates how ZBT, with its emphasis on avoiding preconceived notions and encouraging open-mindedness, can contribute to the development of a vibrant culture of innovation within an organization. Such cultures are essential for staying competitive and responsive in dynamic industries.

Enhancing Problem-Solving

Enhancing problem-solving is a key benefit of Zero-Based Thinking (ZBT), as it encourages individuals and teams to approach challenges with open minds and objectivity. This can lead to more effective and creative problem-solving processes. Here are key aspects to consider:

Objective Analysis: ZBT promotes objective analysis of problems by setting aside preconceived notions and biases. This allows individuals to assess situations more accurately and make decisions based on facts rather than personal beliefs.

Diverse Perspectives: When preconceived notions are avoided, teams can consider a wider range of perspectives and ideas. This diversity of thought often leads to more comprehensive problem-solving approaches.

Innovative Solutions: The willingness to explore unconventional solutions is a hallmark of ZBT. This can lead to the discovery of innovative approaches that might not have been considered otherwise.

Data-Driven Decision-Making: ZBT encourages data-driven decision-making in problem-solving. Instead of relying solely on intuition or habit, individuals gather and analyze relevant data to inform their decisions.

Adaptability: ZBT supports adaptability in problem-solving. As new information becomes available or circumstances change, individuals are more willing to adjust their approaches and solutions.

Example

Let's consider how ZBT enhances problem-solving in the context of a marketing team working for a retail company:

Problem: The retail company is experiencing a decline in foot traffic to its physical stores, and online sales are not growing as expected. The marketing team wants to address this challenge effectively.

With the adoption of ZBT principles, the marketing team approaches the problem-solving process as follows:

Setting Aside Assumptions: The team begins by acknowledging that traditional marketing strategies might not be sufficient. They set aside assumptions such as "traditional advertising methods always work" or "online sales will naturally increase."

Objective Analysis: The team conducts an objective analysis of the problem. They gather data on customer behavior, competitive landscape, and market trends to gain a clear understanding of the factors contributing to the decline in foot traffic and online sales.

Diverse Perspectives: Team members from various backgrounds and roles come together to discuss potential solutions. They encourage input from both digital and in-store marketing specialists, as well as customer service representatives who have direct interactions with customers.

Innovative Solutions: Instead of simply increasing the budget for online advertising, the team explores unconventional solutions. They consider strategies like creating augmented reality experiences in stores, gamifying the shopping experience, and leveraging user-generated content in online campaigns.

Data-Driven Decision-Making: The team uses data to prioritize potential solutions based on their expected impact and feasibility. They analyze the cost-effectiveness of each strategy and its potential to address the problem.

Adaptability: Recognizing that consumer behavior can change rapidly, the team commits to ongoing monitoring and adjustment of their marketing strategies. They set key performance indicators (KPIs) to track progress and adapt their approaches as needed.

As a result of applying ZBT to enhance problem-solving, the marketing team achieves several outcomes:

They develop innovative marketing campaigns that capture the attention of both online and in-store shoppers.

The decline in foot traffic stabilizes, and online sales show signs of growth.

The team becomes more agile in responding to changes in consumer behavior and market dynamics.

Marketing strategies are based on data and evidence, leading to more informed decision-making.

The company's overall competitiveness improves as a result of more effective problem-solving.

This example demonstrates how ZBT's approach to problem-solving, by encouraging objective analysis, diversity of thought, and innovative solutions, can lead to more effective and adaptive problem-solving processes within an organization. It emphasizes the value of open-mindedness and data-driven decision-making in achieving successful outcomes.

Resource Allocation

Zero-Based Thinking's approach to resource allocation in a business context is about transforming budgeting into a strategic and dynamic process. By requiring a justification for every expense and emphasizing value and strategic alignment, ZBT helps organizations make more informed, efficient, and adaptable decisions regarding the allocation of their resources.

Budgeting as a Strategic Exercise

Budgeting is a critical process for individuals and organizations to allocate resources effectively and achieve financial goals. ZBT elevates budgeting from a routine or incremental task to a strategic one by requiring a comprehensive reassessment of every expense. Here are key aspects to consider:

Strategic Alignment: ZBT emphasizes the importance of aligning the budget with the broader goals and objectives of the organization. It ensures that every expenditure serves a strategic purpose and contributes to the company's mission.

Thorough Evaluation: Unlike traditional budgeting, which may start with the previous year's budget as a baseline, ZBT mandates a thorough evaluation of each expense item, requiring justification from scratch. This rigorous assessment eliminates any complacency associated with carrying over past expenses.

Resource Optimization: ZBT prompts organizations to allocate resources based on necessity and value rather than historical precedent. It encourages the reallocation of resources to areas where they can have the most significant impact.

Cost Control: By scrutinizing every expense, ZBT helps identify inefficiencies and cost-saving opportunities. This leads to a more efficient allocation of resources and better cost control.

Flexibility: ZBT recognizes that business conditions can change rapidly. It encourages a flexible approach to budgeting, where adjustments can be made in response to shifts in the economic or competitive landscape.

Example

Let's consider an example of budgeting as a strategic exercise within a manufacturing company:

A manufacturing company has traditionally followed an incremental budgeting process. Each year, they start with the previous year's budget and make minor adjustments based on factors like inflation and expected growth. This approach has worked reasonably well, but the company's leadership believes that they can achieve greater efficiency and alignment with strategic goals through ZBT.

Here's how ZBT transforms their budgeting process:

Comprehensive Expense Review: The company's finance team conducts a comprehensive review of all expenses, starting with personnel costs. Instead of assuming that all existing positions are necessary, they assess staffing levels based on current workloads and strategic priorities.

Supplier Relationships: The procurement department reevaluates supplier relationships, negotiating new contracts and terms with the aim of reducing costs while maintaining product quality.

Marketing and Sales: The marketing and sales teams are challenged to justify their budgets based on expected returns and alignment with the company's growth objectives. This includes exploring new marketing channels and approaches.

Technology Investments: The IT department reviews its technology investments, ensuring that software and hardware expenses support the company's digital transformation initiatives and long-term strategy.

R&D and Innovation: The company increases its budget for research and development, recognizing the importance of innovation in maintaining competitiveness. This includes allocating resources to explore new product lines and technologies.

Risk Assessment: ZBT prompts the company to consider potential risks and uncertainties in their budgeting process.

[57]

They establish contingency plans for unforeseen events that could impact revenue or expenses.

As a result of adopting ZBT principles in their budgeting process, the manufacturing company achieves several benefits:

They identify areas where resources were previously allocated inefficiently and redirect those resources to strategic initiatives.

The budget is more closely aligned with the company's long-term objectives, promoting growth and competitiveness.

The company becomes more agile and responsive to changing market conditions due to its flexible budgeting approach.

Cost savings are realized without compromising product quality or customer satisfaction.

This example illustrates how ZBT's transformation of budgeting into a strategic exercise can lead to more efficient resource allocation, greater alignment with organizational goals, and improved financial performance. It underscores the importance of continually reevaluating expenses to adapt to evolving business environments.

Justifying Every Expense

Justifying every expense is a fundamental principle of ZBT, and it requires that every expenditure, regardless of its historical presence in the budget, must be thoroughly justified. This practice promotes financial discipline, accountability, and the efficient allocation of resources. Here are key aspects to consider:

Accountability: ZBT instills a sense of accountability among budget owners and decision-makers. They are required to provide a clear and well-reasoned justification for each expense they propose or approve.

Eliminating Complacency: Traditional budgeting processes can lead to complacency, where expenses are carried over from year to year without scrutiny. ZBT breaks this cycle by challenging the assumption that existing expenses are automatically necessary.

Strategic Alignment: ZBT ensures that every expense aligns with the strategic goals and priorities of the organization. It prevents resources from being allocated to activities or items that do not contribute to the organization's mission.

Cost Control: By mandating a rigorous justification process, ZBT helps organizations identify unnecessary or redundant costs. This, in turn, supports cost control efforts and can lead to cost savings.

Resource Optimization: ZBT encourages the reallocation of resources to areas where they can have the most significant impact. It prevents resources from being tied up in activities that no longer provide sufficient value.

Example

Let's consider an example of justifying every expense within a marketing department of a retail company:

The marketing department of a retail company has traditionally followed a budgeting process where the previous year's marketing budget was used as a starting point. This process often resulted in budget items that were carried over without a thorough review of their effectiveness. The department decides to implement ZBT principles to ensure that every expense is justified:

Advertising Costs: The marketing team is required to justify each advertising campaign's cost by providing data on expected returns on investment (ROI). For instance, if they plan to spend a significant amount on a television ad campaign, they must present research indicating how this campaign will reach the target audience and lead to increased sales.

Social Media Advertising: Similarly, expenditures on social media advertising are scrutinized. The team must demonstrate how their spending on social media platforms aligns with the company's overall marketing strategy and goals.

Marketing Software: The department uses various marketing software tools. Instead of automatically renewing licenses, they conduct a cost-benefit analysis to determine which tools are essential and which may be redundant or underutilized.

Marketing Events: The team justifies the budget allocated for marketing events and conferences. They must outline the specific benefits, such as networking opportunities or lead generation, that will result from attending each event.

Agency Contracts: If the department engages marketing agencies, the contracts are reviewed to ensure they provide value and align with the company's marketing objectives.

Printed Materials: Expenses related to printed marketing materials, such as brochures or flyers, are assessed for their relevance in the digital age. The team considers whether printed materials still effectively reach the target audience or if alternative digital channels would be more cost-effective.

By implementing ZBT's principle of justifying every expense, the marketing department undergoes a comprehensive review of its budget. This process not only eliminates unnecessary costs but also aligns the budget more closely with the company's strategic marketing goals. As a result, the department becomes more cost-effective and efficient in its marketing efforts, ultimately contributing to the company's bottom line.

This example demonstrates how ZBT's emphasis on justifying expenses promotes financial responsibility and ensures that resources are allocated to activities that generate the most value for the organization.

Enhancing Cost Control

Cost control is a critical aspect of financial management for organizations of all sizes. ZBT is particularly effective in this regard as it promotes a thorough examination of every expense, leading to better financial discipline, frugality, and responsible spending. Here are key aspects to consider:

Granular Expense Review: ZBT requires organizations to scrutinize each expense at a granular level. This means that even small or seemingly insignificant expenses are subject to evaluation, ensuring that no cost goes unchecked.

Identification of Inefficiencies: Through the rigorous review process, ZBT helps organizations identify areas of inefficiency, redundancy, or waste. These inefficiencies can be addressed to streamline operations and reduce costs.

Eliminating Unnecessary Expenses: ZBT encourages the elimination of unnecessary or non-essential expenses. By challenging the assumption that all existing expenses are vital, organizations can reduce their overall spending.

Responsible Spending: ZBT instills a culture of responsible spending within an organization. It encourages employees to consider the necessity and value of each expense, fostering a of ownership and accountability.

Resource Reallocation: By identifying and eliminating inefficient expenses, organizations can reallocate resources to areas where they can have a more significant impact or align with strategic priorities.

Example

Let's consider an example of how ZBT enhances cost control within a manufacturing company:

A manufacturing company has been facing cost overruns and declining profitability in recent years. Traditional budgeting practices have allowed certain expenses to continue unchecked. To regain control over costs, the company decides to implement ZBT principles:

Production Costs: The company closely examines its production costs, including raw materials, labor, and machinery maintenance. They identify areas where cost-saving measures can be implemented, such as negotiating better supplier contracts or improving production efficiency.

Inventory Management: ZBT prompts the company to evaluate its inventory management practices. They discover that excessive stock levels are tying up capital and incurring storage costs. Adjustments are made to optimize inventory levels and reduce carrying costs.

Energy Consumption: The company reviews its energy consumption patterns and identifies opportunities to reduce energy costs. This includes implementing energy-efficient technologies and practices in their manufacturing processes.

Overhead Expenses: The overhead expenses, such as office space, utilities, and administrative costs, are subjected to scrutiny. The company explores options for reducing office space, implementing remote work policies, and renegotiating utility contracts.

Marketing Expenses: The marketing department's budget is assessed, and the effectiveness of various marketing channels is evaluated. The company identifies which channels generate the best ROI and reallocates funds accordingly.

Employee Training: The company invests in employee training to enhance their skills and productivity. This training is seen as an investment that can lead to cost savings through improved efficiency.

By applying ZBT's principles of enhancing cost control, the manufacturing company successfully addresses its cost-related challenges:

Production costs are reduced through negotiations with suppliers and process improvements.

Inventory levels are optimized, freeing up capital and reducing storage costs.

Energy consumption is lowered through the adoption of energy-efficient technologies.

Overhead expenses are trimmed through space reduction and cost-effective administrative practices.

Marketing expenses are redirected to the most effective channels, maximizing ROI.

Employee training leads to improved productivity and efficiency.

As a result, the company regains profitability and financial stability by implementing ZBT's cost control principles. This example illustrates how ZBT's meticulous scrutiny of expenses and commitment to responsible spending can lead to significant cost savings and improved financial performance for organizations.

Prioritization of Resources

Prioritization of resources is a crucial aspect of resource allocation and strategic planning. ZBT emphasizes the need for organizations to allocate resources based on strategic importance and value rather than historical precedents. Here are key aspects to consider:

Strategic Alignment: ZBT aligns resource allocation with an organization's strategic goals and objectives. It ensures that resources are directed toward activities and initiatives that directly contribute to the company's mission and long-term success.

Resource Optimization: By prioritizing resources, ZBT helps organizations optimize the use of their available resources, whether it's financial, human, or time-related. It prevents the dispersion of resources across numerous low-impact activities.

Eliminating Non-Essential Expenses: ZBT encourages organizations to identify and eliminate non-essential or low-value expenses. This frees up resources that can be reallocated to more critical areas.

Efficiency and Effectiveness: Prioritization ensures that resources are allocated efficiently and effectively. It minimizes the risk of overspending on less impactful activities while underinvesting in critical ones.

Adaptability: ZBT recognizes that priorities can change over time due to shifts in the business environment. It encourages organizations to be adaptable and adjust resource allocation as needed to stay aligned with evolving priorities.

Example

Let's consider an example of how ZBT prompts the prioritization of resources within a technology company:

A technology company is experiencing rapid growth and expansion into new markets. In the past, they allocated resources based on historical patterns, with each department receiving a portion of the budget based on previous years' allocations. This approach has become unsustainable as the company grows.

Implementing ZBT, the company takes a more strategic approach to resource prioritization:

Market Expansion: The company's top strategic priority is expanding into new international markets. They allocate a significant portion of their resources to market research, market entry strategies, and hiring international sales and marketing teams.

Product Development: Recognizing that product innovation is a key driver of growth, the company prioritizes its product development efforts. They allocate resources to research and development teams, ensuring they have the tools and talent needed to create cutting-edge products.

Customer Support: Customer satisfaction is critical to retaining existing customers and attracting new ones. The company increases its investment in customer support teams and resources to provide exceptional service.

Marketing: The marketing department receives a budget allocation based on the expected impact of various marketing initiatives. High-ROI campaigns and strategies receive more resources, while less effective channels are deprioritized.

Cost Control: While allocating resources to growth initiatives, the company also invests in cost control measures to ensure that resources are used efficiently and that expenses are justified.

As a result of this strategic prioritization of resources, the technology company achieves several benefits:

They successfully expand into new international markets, capturing a broader customer base.

Product innovation leads to the development of market-leading products that attract new customers.

Exceptional customer support strengthens customer loyalty and retention rates.

Marketing efforts are focused on high-impact campaigns, maximizing ROI.

Cost control measures prevent overspending and ensure resource efficiency.

This example illustrates how ZBT's emphasis on prioritizing resources based on strategic importance and value enables organizations to make more informed and impactful resource allocation decisions. It ensures that resources are directed toward activities that drive growth, innovation, and long-term success.

Resource Reallocation

Resource reallocation is a dynamic aspect of resource management, and ZBT places a strong emphasis on it. This approach encourages organizations to be agile in shifting resources based on evolving priorities, market conditions, or emerging opportunities. Here are key aspects to consider:

Strategic Flexibility: ZBT recognizes that organizational priorities can change over time due to shifts in the business environment. It encourages organizations to have the strategic flexibility to reallocate resources in response to these changes.

Adaptation to Market Shifts: In today's rapidly changing business landscape, market conditions can change swiftly. ZBT allows organizations to reallocate resources to seize new opportunities or pivot in response to challenges.

Efficiency Maximization: Resource reallocation ensures that funds are allocated where they can have the most significant strategic impact. It minimizes the risk of resource stagnation in areas that no longer align with organizational goals.

Risk Mitigation: By enabling swift resource reallocation, ZBT helps organizations mitigate risks associated with overspending in low-impact areas and underinvesting in high-impact ones.

Evidence-Based Decisions: ZBT requires evidence-based decision-making when reallocating resources. Decisions are made based on data, analysis, and a clear understanding of the potential impact on the organization's goals.

Example

Let's consider an example of how ZBT prompts resource reallocation within a retail company:

A retail company operates a chain of physical stores and an e-commerce platform. Traditionally, they allocated a substantial portion of their budget to maintaining and expanding their physical store presence. However, they notice a significant shift in consumer behavior toward online shopping.

Implementing ZBT, the company decides to reallocate resources to adapt to changing market dynamics:

E-commerce Expansion: Recognizing the growing importance of their e-commerce platform, the company reallocates a significant portion of their budget to enhance their online presence. This includes investments in website optimization, digital marketing, and e-commerce technology.

In-Store Experience Enhancement: While scaling back on physical store expansion, the company reallocates resources to enhance the in-store shopping experience. They invest in store renovations, improved customer service training, and interactive displays to attract and retain in-store shoppers.

Supply Chain Optimization: The company recognizes that efficient supply chain management is critical for both online and in-store operations. They reallocate resources to streamline their supply chain processes, reduce lead times, and improve inventory management.

Data Analytics: To make informed decisions about resource allocation, the company invests in data analytics tools and expertise. They allocate resources to gather and analyze customer data, enabling them to tailor their offerings to customer preferences.

Marketing Shift: The company adjusts its marketing budget to allocate more funds to online advertising and customer engagement through digital channels. They reduce spending on traditional advertising methods that have become less effective.

As a result of this resource reallocation based on ZBT principles, the retail company experiences several benefits:

Their e-commerce platform becomes more competitive, attracting a larger online customer base.

In-store improvements enhance the shopping experience, leading to increased foot traffic and customer satisfaction.

Supply chain efficiency reduces costs and improves product availability.

Data-driven decision-making allows the company to tailor their offerings to customer preferences.

Marketing efforts generate better ROI with a focus on digital channels.

This example illustrates how ZBT's approach to resource reallocation enables organizations to respond swiftly to changing market conditions, allocate resources strategically, and remain competitive in a dynamic business environment. It emphasizes the importance of data-driven decisions and adaptability in optimizing resource allocation.

Encouraging Innovation

Encouraging innovation is a significant benefit of ZBT. By requiring teams to justify every expense and explore alternative, cost-effective approaches, ZBT fosters a culture of creativity and forward-thinking. Here are key aspects to consider:

Creative Problem-Solving: ZBT encourages teams to think creatively and find innovative solutions to challenges. It prompts them to question conventional methods and explore new ways of achieving their goals.

Cost-Effective Approaches: Teams are motivated to find cost-effective alternatives to expensive processes or technologies. This can lead to cost savings and increased efficiency.

Process Improvement: The justification process often involves a close examination of existing processes. Teams can identify bottlenecks, redundancies, or areas for improvement, leading to streamlined operations.

Technology Innovation: Teams may explore new technologies or tools that can provide better value for their budget. This can result in the adoption of innovative technologies that improve productivity or customer experiences.

Business Model Innovation: ZBT can lead to the reevaluation of an organization's business model. Teams may identify opportunities to pivot or diversify their offerings to better meet customer needs.

Example

Let's consider an example of how ZBT encourages innovation within a technology company's product development department:

A technology company is developing a new software application. Traditionally, their product development process followed a set path that involved extensive research and development expenditures. With the adoption of ZBT, the product development team is encouraged to innovate and find more cost-effective ways to bring their product to market:

Lean Development: Instead of investing heavily in developing all features of the software upfront, the team adopts a lean development approach. They prioritize the core features and launch a minimum viable product (MVP) to gather user feedback and refine the product based on real-world usage.

Cloud Services: The team explores the use of cloud services for hosting the software, eliminating the need to invest in expensive physical infrastructure. This approach reduces initial costs and allows for scalability as the user base grows.

Open-Source Components: To accelerate development, the team leverages open-source libraries and components, reducing the need to build everything from scratch. This not only saves time but also lowers development costs.

User-Centered Design: The team actively engages users in the design process, seeking their input and preferences. This user-centric approach ensures that the product meets user needs effectively, reducing the risk of costly post-launch revisions.

Agile Development: Adopting agile development practices, the team iteratively builds and improves the software based on user feedback. This approach allows for rapid adaptation to changing requirements and market conditions.

As a result of implementing ZBT and fostering innovation, the technology company experiences several benefits:

The software is brought to market more quickly and cost-effectively.

User feedback informs product development, leading to a product that better meets customer needs.

Leveraging open-source components reduces development costs and speeds up the process.

Cloud hosting offers scalability and cost savings.

The company's agile approach allows for continuous improvement and adaptation.

This example illustrates how ZBT's encouragement of innovation can lead to more efficient processes, cost-effective solutions, and products that better align with customer needs. It emphasizes the importance of creativity and adaptability in achieving organizational goals.

Transparency and Accountability

Transparency and accountability are fundamental principles of effective financial management, and ZBT reinforces these principles by requiring thorough justification for every expense. This practice promotes a culture of openness, responsibility, and efficient resource utilization. Here are key aspects to consider:

Clear Responsibility: ZBT makes it clear who is responsible for each line item in the budget. Budget owners and decision-makers are accountable for justifying and managing the expenses under their purview.

Open Communication: The requirement to justify expenses encourages open and honest communication within an organization. It creates a dialogue where team members can discuss the necessity and value of each expense.

Resource Stewardship: ZBT encourages individuals and teams to be good stewards of organizational resources. It fosters a sense of ownership and responsibility for ensuring that resources are used efficiently and responsibly.

Alignment with Goals: By linking expenses to strategic objectives, ZBT ensures that every expenditure serves a clear purpose and contributes to the organization's mission.

Data-Driven Decisions: Transparent justifications for expenses are based on data and analysis, ensuring that decisions are made with a clear understanding of their impact on the organization's financial health.

Example

Let's consider an example of how ZBT promotes transparency and accountability within a nonprofit organization's program management:

[74]

A nonprofit organization is responsible for delivering various programs to support its mission. Traditionally, the organization allocated resources to each program based on historical funding levels. With the adoption of ZBT, they implement a more transparent and accountable approach:

Program Justification: Program managers are required to provide a detailed justification for the resources allocated to their programs. This includes outlining program goals, expected outcomes, and the specific impact on the organization's mission.

Budget Review Committee: The organization establishes a budget review committee composed of key stakeholders. This committee reviews and evaluates program justifications to ensure alignment with the organization's strategic goals.

Resource Reallocation: The committee has the authority to reallocate resources among programs based on their impact and alignment with the mission. If a program's impact is not well-justified, resources may be shifted to programs with clearer objectives and outcomes.

Regular Reporting: Program managers provide regular reports on their programs' progress and outcomes. This transparency allows stakeholders to monitor the effectiveness of resource allocation and program performance.

Continuous Improvement: The organization encourages a culture of continuous improvement, where program managers are open to feedback and willing to adapt their strategies based on data and results.

As a result of implementing ZBT principles, the nonprofit organization experiences several benefits:

Resources are allocated to programs with the greatest impact on the organization's mission.

Accountability is clear, with program managers responsible for justifying their budgets and outcomes.

The organization fosters a culture of transparency and open communication among stakeholders.

Regular reporting ensures that resources are used efficiently and effectively.

Programs are more adaptable and responsive to changing community needs.

This example illustrates how ZBT's emphasis on transparency and accountability ensures that resources are used responsibly and that organizational goals are consistently aligned with mission-driven outcomes. It underscores the importance of clear communication and data-driven decision-making in promoting transparency and accountability.

Continuous Improvement

Continuous improvement is a core principle of ZBT that encourages organizations to view resource allocation as an evolving process rather than a static one. It emphasizes the need to continually assess and adjust resource allocation strategies based on changing conditions, emerging opportunities, and new information. Here are key aspects to consider:

Adaptability: ZBT promotes a culture of adaptability where organizations can respond quickly to changing circumstances. It recognizes that business environments are dynamic, and resource allocation should be flexible to remain effective.

Data-Driven Decision-Making: Continuous improvement relies on data and evidence to inform resource allocation decisions. Organizations collect and analyze data to assess the impact of resource allocation strategies and identify areas for enhancement.

Feedback Loops: ZBT encourages the establishment of feedback mechanisms that allow stakeholders to provide input and insights into resource allocation decisions. This promotes collaboration and helps identify opportunities for improvement.

Alignment with Goals: Continuous improvement ensures that resource allocation remains aligned with organizational goals and objectives. If priorities shift, resource allocation strategies can be adjusted accordingly.

Efficiency Enhancement: By regularly reviewing and optimizing resource allocation, organizations can identify inefficiencies and redundancies, leading to cost savings and improved efficiency.

Example

Let's consider an example of how continuous improvement is applied within a manufacturing company's production processes using ZBT principles:

A manufacturing company produces consumer electronics. Traditionally, the company allocated resources to its production processes based on historical practices and industry standards. With the adoption of ZBT, they implement a continuous improvement approach:

Data Collection: The company starts by collecting data on various aspects of production, including cycle times, defect rates, and equipment utilization. This data is regularly updated and analyzed.

Resource Allocation Review: The production manager and a cross-functional team regularly review resource allocation within the manufacturing process. They assess whether current resource levels are aligned with production goals and customer demand.

Feedback from Operators: Operators on the production floor are encouraged to provide feedback on resource allocation. They can highlight bottlenecks, suggest process improvements, or identify equipment maintenance needs.

Resource Reallocation: Based on data analysis and feedback, the company identifies areas for resource reallocation. For instance, they may shift resources to a specific production line that consistently experiences higher demand.

Process Optimization: Continuous improvement also involves process optimization. The company regularly evaluates production workflows and makes adjustments to improve efficiency, reduce waste, and enhance product quality.

Investment in Technology: If data analysis indicates that certain equipment is becoming a bottleneck, the company may invest in automation or upgraded machinery to enhance production capacity.

Over time, this continuous improvement approach leads to several benefits for the manufacturing company:

Improved production efficiency and reduced cycle times.

Enhanced product quality and reduced defect rates.

Better alignment of resource allocation with production demand.

Increased agility to respond to fluctuations in customer orders.

Cost savings through resource optimization and process improvements.

This example demonstrates how ZBT's emphasis on continuous improvement in resource allocation enables organizations to adapt to changing conditions, streamline processes, and achieve greater efficiency and effectiveness. It underscores the value of data-driven decision-making and feedback loops in driving ongoing improvement efforts.

Alignment with Strategy

Alignment with strategy is a fundamental principle of ZBT that emphasizes the importance of ensuring that resource allocation decisions are closely tied to an organization's strategic priorities and long-term goals. Here are key aspects to consider:

Strategic Clarity: ZBT requires organizations to have a clear understanding of their strategic objectives. It prompts leadership to articulate and communicate the organization's mission, vision, and goals effectively.
Resource Allocation Prioritization: Resources are allocated to activities and initiatives that directly support the strategic priorities. ZBT ensures that every expense is evaluated in the context of how it contributes to the organization's overall strategy.

Strategic Flexibility: ZBT recognizes that strategies can evolve in response to changing market conditions or new opportunities. It encourages organizations to have the flexibility to reallocate resources in alignment with shifting strategic priorities.

Goal Achievement: The alignment of resource allocation with strategy increases the likelihood of achieving long-term goals. It minimizes the risk of resource dispersion across activities that do not significantly contribute to the organization's mission.

Measurement and Evaluation: ZBT emphasizes the importance of performance measurement and evaluation. Organizations regularly assess how resource allocation decisions impact progress toward strategic objectives.

Example

Let's consider an example of how ZBT promotes alignment with strategy within a technology startup:

A technology startup is focused on developing innovative software solutions for the healthcare industry. To ensure alignment with its strategic goals, the startup adopts ZBT principles:

Strategic Priorities: The startup's leadership identifies its strategic priorities, including product development, market expansion, and customer acquisition in the healthcare sector.

Resource Allocation Review: On a quarterly basis, the startup conducts a comprehensive review of resource allocation. They assess how financial resources, human capital, and time are allocated across various activities.

Alignment Assessment: Each allocation is assessed for alignment with strategic priorities. For instance, if a significant portion of the budget is dedicated to research and development, the startup ensures that these activities are directly linked to the development of healthcare software solutions.

Reallocation for Growth: As the startup gains insights from the market, it may decide to shift resources from one product line to another if there is a greater growth potential in a specific healthcare subsector.

Measuring Progress: The startup continually monitors its progress toward strategic goals, using key performance indicators (KPIs) to evaluate the impact of resource allocation decisions on product development timelines, customer acquisition rates, and market penetration.

Strategic Pivot: If the startup identifies a new opportunity, such as a partnership with a healthcare provider, it has the flexibility to pivot its strategy and reallocate resources to seize this opportunity.

By aligning resource allocation with its strategic priorities using ZBT, the technology startup realizes several benefits:

Efficient use of resources to accelerate product development in the healthcare sector.

Increased focus on activities that directly contribute to customer acquisition and market expansion.

Flexibility to adapt to changing market conditions and emerging opportunities.

Enhanced decision-making based on measurable progress toward strategic objectives.

Improved chances of achieving long-term success in the healthcare industry.

This example illustrates how ZBT's emphasis on alignment with strategy enables organizations to focus their resources on activities that are essential for achieving their mission and vision. It highlights the importance of regular reviews and reallocation to ensure alignment with changing priorities and market dynamics.

Efficiency and Innovation

Zero-Based Thinking's impact on efficiency and innovation is significant. By challenging existing practices and emphasizing the need to justify expenses and allocate resources effectively, ZBT drives organizations to become leaner, more agile, and more innovative, ultimately enhancing their competitiveness and sustainability. It promotes a dynamic and forward-thinking approach to problem-solving and resource management.

Efficiency through Scrutiny

Efficiency through scrutiny is a fundamental principle of Zero-Based Thinking (ZBT) that emphasizes the importance of thoroughly evaluating and optimizing every aspect of an organization's operations. This critical examination often leads to the discovery of inefficiencies and opportunities for improvement. Here are key aspects to consider:

Challenging the Status Quo: ZBT encourages organizations to challenge established practices and assumptions. It prompts them to question whether current methods are truly the most efficient, even if they have been in place for a long time.

Bottleneck Identification: Through scrutiny, organizations can identify bottlenecks or areas where processes slow down or become less efficient. Identifying and addressing these bottlenecks can lead to significant productivity improvements.

Redundancy Elimination: ZBT helps organizations recognize and eliminate redundancies in workflows or resource allocation. Reducing duplication of efforts or resources can result in cost savings and streamlined operations.

Continuous Improvement: The scrutiny process is ongoing, promoting a culture of continuous improvement. Organizations regularly reassess their operations to ensure that they remain efficient and aligned with their goals.

Resource Optimization: Resource allocation is evaluated with a focus on optimizing the use of available resources. This includes financial resources, human capital, time, and technology.

Example

Let's consider how ZBT enhances efficiency through scrutiny within a manufacturing company:

[86]

Challenge: The manufacturing company has been experiencing production delays and increased production costs. To address these challenges, they adopt ZBT principles to improve efficiency.

Process Evaluation: The company begins by evaluating its production processes from start to finish. This includes material sourcing, manufacturing, quality control, and shipping.

Bottleneck Identification: During the scrutiny process, they identify a bottleneck in the assembly line caused by a manual inspection process. This manual inspection is time-consuming and error-prone.

Redundancy Elimination: They discover that some raw materials are ordered from multiple suppliers, leading to redundant inventory and increased procurement costs. By consolidating suppliers and streamlining the procurement process, they aim to reduce redundancy.

Resource Allocation Review: The company reviews its resource allocation, reallocating labor resources to address the bottleneck and investing in automated quality control systems to reduce manual inspections.

Continuous Improvement: Regular performance metrics are established to monitor production efficiency, defect rates, and cost savings. The company commits to ongoing process improvement, seeking to further optimize operations.

As a result of implementing ZBT principles to enhance efficiency through scrutiny, the manufacturing company experiences several benefits:

Production delays are reduced, allowing them to fulfill customer orders more efficiently.

Manufacturing costs decrease due to streamlined processes and reduced labor requirements.

[87]

Inventory and procurement costs are lowered through supplier consolidation and improved procurement practices.

The company establishes a culture of continuous improvement, which leads to ongoing efficiency gains.

This example illustrates how ZBT's emphasis on scrutinizing existing practices and processes can lead to significant efficiency improvements within an organization. It highlights the importance of identifying bottlenecks, eliminating redundancies, and optimizing resource allocation to enhance operational efficiency.

Leaner Operations

Leaner operations are a valuable outcome of Zero-Based Thinking (ZBT) as it encourages organizations to evaluate their processes rigorously and make decisions based on their value and efficiency. The goal is to eliminate or streamline activities that no longer provide adequate value relative to their costs. Here are key aspects to consider:

Value-Cost Analysis: ZBT prompts organizations to conduct a thorough analysis of the value provided by each process or activity relative to its associated costs. This analysis is crucial for identifying areas that may be candidates for elimination or optimization.

Resource Optimization: When organizations identify processes that are less efficient or too costly compared to their value, they can reallocate resources more effectively. This may involve reallocating manpower, technology, or financial resources to more value-generating activities.

Streamlining: ZBT encourages organizations to streamline processes to reduce waste, unnecessary steps, and inefficiencies. Streamlining can lead to smoother workflows and cost savings.

Focus on Core Competencies: By eliminating non-core or low-value activities, organizations can focus more on their core competencies and strategic priorities. This can lead to increased competitiveness and improved overall performance.

Example

Let's explore how ZBT leads to leaner operations within a logistics company:

Challenge: The logistics company, responsible for transporting goods from manufacturers to retailers, is experiencing rising operational costs and longer delivery times. They adopt ZBT principles to improve efficiency and reduce costs.

Process Evaluation: The company conducts a comprehensive evaluation of its logistics processes, from order placement to delivery. They examine each step to understand where costs are incurred and where value is generated.

Value-Cost Analysis: During the analysis, they identify that a particular step in the delivery process involves multiple manual checks and verifications. While these checks were initially implemented to ensure accuracy, they have become redundant and time-consuming.

Streamlining: Based on their findings, the company decides to streamline the delivery verification process. They implement an automated tracking system that provides real-time updates on shipments and reduces the need for manual checks.

Resource Reallocation: With the streamlined process in place, the company reallocates personnel who were previously responsible for manual verifications to roles that focus on customer service and route optimization.

Cost Reduction: The automation of the verification process reduces labor costs and significantly shortens delivery times. As a result, the company achieves cost savings and improves customer satisfaction.

Focus on Core Competencies: With leaner operations, the logistics company can redirect its efforts toward optimizing routes, managing inventory, and providing value-added services to its clients, aligning more closely with its core competencies.

Through the application of ZBT principles, the logistics company achieves several benefits:

Reduced operational costs and increased efficiency in delivery.

[90]

Improved customer satisfaction due to faster and more reliable services.

Reallocation of human resources to activities that drive value.

Enhanced focus on core competencies and strategic priorities.

Ongoing monitoring and evaluation of processes to maintain lean operations.

This example illustrates how ZBT's focus on value-cost analysis and process optimization can lead to leaner operations within an organization, resulting in cost savings, increased efficiency, and improved competitiveness. It emphasizes the importance of continuously evaluating processes to ensure they align with an organization's strategic goals and provide value.

Resource Optimization

Resource optimization is a central tenet of Zero-Based Thinking (ZBT), emphasizing the importance of allocating resources efficiently to maximize their impact on an organization's strategic priorities. This approach ensures that resources are directed toward activities that align with the organization's goals, thereby preventing waste and enhancing overall performance. Here are key aspects to consider:

Strategic Alignment: ZBT requires organizations to align resource allocation with their strategic objectives and priorities. Every allocation decision is evaluated in the context of how it contributes to achieving long-term goals.

Value-Based Allocation: Resource optimization involves allocating resources to activities that provide the most value and align with the organization's mission. It's about directing resources where they can make the most significant impact.

Resource Reallocation: ZBT promotes the flexibility to reallocate resources based on changing circumstances, market dynamics, or emerging opportunities. This agility allows organizations to respond effectively to evolving needs.

Efficiency Gains: By optimizing resource allocation, organizations can identify areas where they can reduce waste, eliminate redundancies, and enhance cost-effectiveness. This leads to efficiency gains and cost savings.

Example

Let's explore how resource optimization is applied within a technology company:

Challenge: The technology company is known for developing a wide range of software products, but they have been facing resource allocation challenges, including budget overruns and delayed product launches. They adopt ZBT principles to optimize resource allocation.

Strategic Alignment: The leadership team defines clear strategic priorities, including a focus on developing innovative products for a specific target market. These priorities guide all resource allocation decisions.

Value-Based Allocation: The company evaluates its portfolio of software projects and identifies products that are no longer aligned with its strategic priorities or have limited market potential. They decide to discontinue or deprioritize these projects.

Resource Reallocation: With projects deprioritized, the company reallocates development teams, budget, and time to the projects aligned with their strategic priorities. They also invest in research and development to explore new opportunities in the target market.

Efficiency Gains: By discontinuing non-strategic projects and reallocating resources, the company reduces development costs and accelerates product development timelines. This leads to cost savings and improved time-to-market.

Outcome: As a result of resource optimization through ZBT:

The company delivers innovative products tailored to the target market, enhancing competitiveness.

Development teams are more focused, leading to increased productivity and higher-quality products.

Budgets are managed more effectively, preventing budget overruns and aligning expenses with strategic priorities.

The company achieves its strategic objectives more efficiently and cost-effectively.

[93]

This example illustrates how ZBT's resource optimization principles can lead to improved allocation decisions within an organization. By aligning resources with strategic priorities, eliminating non-value-added activities, and fostering flexibility in resource allocation, organizations can enhance their overall performance and achieve their long-term goals more effectively.

Innovation Catalyst

Innovation catalyst is a powerful aspect of Zero-Based Thinking (ZBT) that encourages organizations to leverage the principles of questioning established practices and seeking value in every expense as a means to foster innovation. This approach can lead to creative problem-solving and the development of innovative solutions to longstanding challenges. Here are key aspects to consider:

Questioning the Status Quo: ZBT encourages organizations to question established practices, routines, and processes. This questioning often reveals areas where traditional methods may no longer be the most effective or efficient.

Creative Problem-Solving: Challenging conventional wisdom prompts teams to think creatively about how to solve problems or address challenges. It encourages the exploration of alternative approaches and solutions.

Resource Allocation for Innovation: ZBT enables organizations to allocate resources strategically, directing investments toward innovative projects or initiatives that have the potential to drive growth, competitiveness, or improved performance.

Open-Mindedness: An open-minded approach is essential for fostering innovation. ZBT encourages teams to be receptive to new ideas, even if they contradict existing practices or beliefs.

Continuous Improvement: Innovation is an ongoing process. ZBT emphasizes the importance of continually assessing and refining practices, processes, and resource allocation to foster a culture of continuous innovation.

Example

Let's consider how ZBT acts as an innovation catalyst within a manufacturing company:

Challenge: The manufacturing company has been grappling with high energy costs for its production processes. They decide to apply ZBT principles to address this challenge.

Questioning Established Practices: The company's leadership encourages teams to question long-standing practices related to energy consumption. They ask employees to identify areas where energy is being used inefficiently.

Creative Problem-Solving: Through brainstorming sessions, employees come up with innovative ideas to reduce energy consumption. One idea is to implement energy-efficient lighting and heating systems in the production facility, which would lead to significant cost savings over time.

Resource Allocation for Innovation: Recognizing the potential value in this idea, the company reallocates its budget to invest in upgrading the lighting and heating systems. They also allocate resources for employee training on energy-efficient practices.

Open-Mindedness: The leadership team maintains an open-minded approach to the proposed changes, even though they require upfront investments. They understand that the long-term cost savings and reduced environmental impact make it a worthwhile endeavor.

Continuous Improvement: The company continues to monitor energy consumption and explores additional innovative solutions, such as integrating renewable energy sources or implementing smart energy management systems, to further reduce costs and environmental impact.

As a result of applying ZBT principles as an innovation catalyst, the manufacturing company achieves several outcomes:

Significant reduction in energy costs through the implementation of energy-efficient practices and technologies.

Enhanced competitiveness in the market due to reduced production costs.

A more sustainable and environmentally responsible image, which appeals to customers and investors.

A culture of continuous innovation that encourages employees to proactively seek opportunities for improvement.

This example illustrates how ZBT, with its focus on questioning established practices and seeking value, can act as a catalyst for innovation within an organization. It emphasizes the importance of fostering a culture that encourages creative problem-solving and the development of novel solutions to address challenges and improve overall performance.

Encouraging Risk-Taking

Encouraging risk-taking is an important aspect of Zero-Based Thinking (ZBT) that arises from its emphasis on justifying every expense and seeking efficiency. This approach encourages organizations to take calculated risks in exploring new approaches and technologies, fostering a culture of innovation and potentially leading to breakthrough innovations. Here are key aspects to consider:

Calculated Risk-Taking: ZBT encourages organizations to assess the potential risks and rewards associated with each expense or initiative. This assessment allows them to make informed decisions about whether to invest resources in a particular area, even if it involves some level of uncertainty.

Innovation Through Experimentation: By encouraging calculated risk-taking, ZBT promotes experimentation and exploration of new approaches, technologies, and strategies. It recognizes that not all risks result in failure, and some can lead to significant advancements.

Resource Allocation for Innovation: ZBT enables organizations to allocate resources to support innovative projects or initiatives that carry a certain level of risk but also have the potential for substantial rewards.

Learning from Failure: Embracing risk means accepting that some initiatives may not succeed as expected. However, ZBT promotes a culture of learning from failure, where organizations analyze what went wrong, extract valuable lessons, and apply them to future endeavors.

Example

Let's explore how ZBT encourages risk-taking and innovation within a technology startup:

Challenge: The startup aims to develop a groundbreaking software product that requires cutting-edge technology and significant research and development (R&D) investment. However, the potential risks and uncertainty associated with the project are high.

Calculated Risk Assessment: The startup's leadership conducts a thorough risk assessment, evaluating the potential rewards of developing the groundbreaking software against the associated risks and uncertainties. They recognize that this project aligns with their long-term vision and could be a game-changer in the market.

Resource Allocation for Innovation: The startup decides to allocate a substantial portion of its budget and talent pool to support the R&D efforts required for the project. They also secure external funding from investors who share their vision and appetite for calculated risk.

Innovation Through Experimentation: The project involves experimenting with emerging technologies and untested methodologies. The team explores unconventional solutions and is willing to pivot if initial approaches don't yield the desired results.

Learning from Failure: Along the way, the startup encounters setbacks and challenges. Some experiments fail to produce the expected results. However, instead of viewing these failures as setbacks, they analyze them, adjust their strategies, and apply lessons learned to refine their approach.

Outcome: As a result of embracing calculated risk-taking through ZBT:

The startup successfully develops the groundbreaking software product, which disrupts the market and generates significant revenue.

Investors are pleased with the innovation and long-term potential, leading to additional funding rounds.

The startup's culture of embracing calculated risk and learning from failures becomes a key driver of its continued success in developing innovative products.

This example illustrates how ZBT, by encouraging organizations to assess risks, allocate resources strategically, and embrace innovation through experimentation, can lead to breakthrough innovations that may not have been considered in a more conservative budgeting or resource allocation process. It emphasizes the importance of calculated risk-taking in driving innovation and growth.

Data-Driven Decisions

Data-driven decisions are a fundamental aspect of Zero-Based Thinking (ZBT), emphasizing the importance of relying on data and evidence to justify expenses and allocate resources effectively. This approach ensures that decisions are based on objective analysis rather than assumptions or tradition, ultimately contributing to informed and efficient decision-making. Here are key aspects to consider:

Objective Analysis: ZBT promotes objective analysis by encouraging organizations to rely on data and evidence rather than subjective opinions or assumptions when making decisions.

Data Collection: Organizations collect relevant data and information to assess the value and necessity of each expense or resource allocation. This may involve financial data, performance metrics, market research, and other sources of information.

Performance Metrics: ZBT often involves the establishment of key performance indicators (KPIs) to measure the effectiveness and impact of expenses and resource allocations. These metrics help organizations track progress and make data-driven adjustments.

Informed Decision-Making: Decision-makers use the data and evidence collected to make informed and strategic decisions that align with the organization's goals and priorities.

Continuous Monitoring: ZBT promotes ongoing monitoring of expenses and resource allocations to ensure that they remain aligned with organizational objectives. Data-driven decisions are not limited to initial assessments but extend to regular performance evaluations.

[101]

Example

Let's consider how ZBT encourages data-driven decisions in a retail company's marketing strategy:

Challenge: The retail company is looking to optimize its marketing budget to improve the return on investment (ROI) for its advertising campaigns.

Data Collection: The company begins by collecting data on the performance of its previous marketing campaigns. They gather information on customer engagement, conversion rates, sales generated, and the cost of each campaign.

Objective Analysis: Using the collected data, the marketing team objectively evaluates the performance of each advertising channel and campaign. They identify which campaigns have consistently delivered a positive ROI and which have not.

Performance Metrics: The team establishes KPIs, such as customer acquisition cost (CAC) and customer lifetime value (CLV), to measure the effectiveness of marketing campaigns in terms of revenue generation and long-term customer value.

Informed Decision-Making: Based on the data and performance metrics, the marketing team makes informed decisions about where to allocate their marketing budget. They decide to reallocate funds from underperforming campaigns to those with a proven track record of delivering a positive ROI.

Continuous Monitoring: The marketing team continues to monitor the performance of campaigns, using data to track changes in ROI and customer engagement. They adjust their resource allocation as needed to maximize marketing efficiency.

As a result of adopting ZBT's data-driven approach to marketing decisions:

The retail company achieves a higher ROI on its marketing budget, as resources are directed toward campaigns that consistently generate revenue.

Customer acquisition costs decrease, leading to more cost-effective customer acquisition strategies.

The marketing team's decisions are aligned with the organization's goal of improving profitability and efficiency.

This example demonstrates how ZBT's emphasis on data-driven decisions enables organizations to optimize resource allocation and make informed choices that enhance performance and achieve strategic objectives. It underscores the value of using data and evidence to guide decision-making processes.

Culture of Continuous Improvement

A culture of continuous improvement is a key element of Zero-Based Thinking (ZBT) that encourages organizations to regularly reassess their processes, resource allocation strategies, and decision-making approaches. This culture places a strong emphasis on seeking ongoing enhancements and efficiencies rather than resting on past successes. Here are key aspects to consider:

Regular Evaluation: ZBT fosters a mindset where organizations routinely evaluate their operations, expenses, and resource allocation strategies. This evaluation isn't limited to a one-time exercise but is integrated into the organization's ongoing processes.

Adaptability: Organizations that embrace continuous improvement are more adaptable and responsive to changes in their internal and external environments. They proactively identify areas that require adjustment and adapt their strategies accordingly.

Learning from Experience: Continuous improvement involves learning from both successes and failures. Organizations analyze the results of past decisions, extract valuable lessons, and apply them to future endeavors.

Efficiency Enhancement: The goal of continuous improvement is to enhance efficiency, effectiveness, and overall performance. This can result in cost savings, streamlined processes, and improved customer satisfaction.

Cultural Shift: Embracing continuous improvement often requires a cultural shift within an organization. It encourages employees at all levels to contribute ideas for improvement and fosters an environment where innovation is valued.

Example

Let's explore how ZBT promotes a culture of continuous improvement within a manufacturing company:

Challenge: The manufacturing company has been experiencing production delays and rising production costs. They recognize the need for a culture of continuous improvement to address these challenges.

Regular Evaluation: The company establishes a regular process for evaluating its production processes, including a cross-functional team responsible for assessing operations, identifying bottlenecks, and recommending improvements.

Learning from Experience: The team reviews historical data on production delays and cost overruns. They analyze past incidents to understand the root causes of issues and extract lessons that can inform future decisions.

Efficiency Enhancement: Based on their assessments, the team identifies several areas for improvement, including the implementation of automated quality control systems, revised production schedules, and additional training for staff.

Cultural Shift: The company fosters a culture where employees at all levels are encouraged to contribute improvement ideas. Suggestions are actively sought, and teams are empowered to implement changes that enhance efficiency.

Adaptability: The cross-functional team continuously monitors production processes and adjusts strategies based on real-time data and feedback. They remain adaptable and responsive to changes in production demands and market dynamics.

As a result of adopting ZBT's culture of continuous improvement:

Production delays are significantly reduced, leading to improved on-time delivery performance.

Production costs decrease due to streamlined processes and reduced waste.

Employee engagement and satisfaction increase as their input is valued and incorporated into improvements.

The organization becomes more agile and responsive to changing market demands.

This example illustrates how ZBT's promotion of continuous improvement can lead to enhanced efficiency, adaptability, and overall performance within an organization. It emphasizes the importance of regular evaluation, learning from experience, and fostering a culture that values innovation and ongoing enhancement.

Competitive Advantage

Achieving a competitive advantage is a significant outcome of embracing Zero-Based Thinking (ZBT) principles. Organizations that implement ZBT often find themselves better positioned to adapt to changing market conditions, deliver products or services more efficiently, and innovate faster, which collectively contribute to their competitiveness in their respective industries. Here are key aspects to consider:

Adaptation to Market Changes: ZBT encourages organizations to regularly reassess their strategies and resource allocation. This adaptability enables them to respond swiftly to shifts in customer preferences, emerging trends, or economic fluctuations.

Efficient Resource Allocation: By scrutinizing expenses and resource allocation, organizations can eliminate waste and direct resources toward activities that provide the most value. This efficiency leads to cost savings and improved cost structures.

Innovation and Creativity: ZBT fosters a culture of innovation by challenging established practices and encouraging open-mindedness. This culture often leads to the development of new products, services, and processes that set organizations apart from competitors.

Agility: Organizations that embrace ZBT are typically more agile in decision-making and resource allocation. This agility allows them to seize opportunities quickly and respond to competitive threats.

Continuous Improvement: ZBT promotes a culture of continuous improvement, where organizations actively seek ways to enhance their operations and strategies. This ongoing process keeps them ahead of competitors who may rely on more static approaches.

Example

Let's explore how a tech startup achieves a competitive advantage through ZBT:

Challenge: The tech startup operates in a rapidly evolving industry where customer demands and technology trends change quickly. To thrive in this environment, they adopt ZBT principles.

Adaptation to Market Changes: The startup regularly monitors market trends and customer feedback. When they notice a shift in customer preferences toward a particular technology solution, they are quick to pivot their product development efforts in that direction.

Efficient Resource Allocation: ZBT prompts the startup to assess the return on investment for various product features and marketing channels continually. They identify which features generate the most user engagement and allocate resources accordingly.

Innovation and Creativity: The company encourages employees to challenge existing product designs and explore new technologies. This open-minded approach leads to the development of innovative features that resonate with users and set the product apart from competitors.

Agility: When a competitor launches a similar product, the startup is agile enough to respond with new features or enhancements quickly. Their decision-making process is streamlined, enabling them to stay ahead in the market.

Continuous Improvement: The startup regularly conducts retrospectives on product launches and marketing campaigns. They gather feedback, analyze what worked and what didn't, and use this information to refine their strategies continually.

As a result of adopting ZBT's principles and achieving a competitive advantage:

The startup maintains a strong position in the market by consistently delivering innovative solutions aligned with customer needs.

Their efficient resource allocation leads to cost-effective operations and a healthier bottom line.

A culture of open-mindedness and continuous improvement drives ongoing innovation and ensures that they stay ahead of competitors.

This example illustrates how ZBT's principles, including adaptation to market changes, efficient resource allocation, innovation, agility, and continuous improvement, collectively contribute to a competitive advantage in a fast-paced industry. It underscores the importance of ZBT in helping organizations remain competitive in dynamic markets.

Environmental Sustainability

Environmental sustainability is a critical outcome of Zero-Based Thinking (ZBT) principles, as it aligns with efforts to reduce waste, optimize resource use, and minimize an organization's environmental footprint. ZBT encourages organizations to think critically about their operations, which often leads to more sustainable practices. Here are key aspects to consider:

Efficiency and Sustainability: ZBT emphasizes the need for efficiency in resource allocation and expense justification. Efficiency inherently leads to reduced resource consumption, which is a core component of sustainability.

Resource Optimization: ZBT prompts organizations to allocate resources more effectively, directing them toward activities that provide value while reducing waste and excess consumption of resources.

Reduction of Environmental Impact: By scrutinizing expenses and processes, organizations can identify opportunities to reduce energy consumption, waste production, and carbon emissions, all of which contribute to a smaller environmental footprint.

Innovation for Sustainability: ZBT's open-minded approach fosters innovation, often leading to the development of environmentally friendly practices, products, and technologies.

Responsibility and Accountability: ZBT promotes a culture of responsibility and accountability in resource allocation. Organizations recognize their role in environmental sustainability and actively seek ways to reduce negative impacts.

Example

Let's explore how a manufacturing company embraces environmental sustainability through ZBT:

Challenge: The manufacturing company faces increasing pressure to reduce its environmental impact and operate more sustainably. They adopt ZBT principles to address this challenge.

Efficiency and Sustainability: The company starts by assessing its production processes and supply chain. They identify inefficiencies that result in excess energy consumption and waste generation.

Resource Optimization: Through ZBT, the company reallocates resources to invest in energy-efficient technologies and processes. They also adopt circular economy practices to reduce waste and increase recycling rates.

Reduction of Environmental Impact: By optimizing resource use, the company significantly reduces its carbon emissions and waste production. They track and report these reductions to demonstrate their commitment to sustainability.

Innovation for Sustainability: The company encourages employees to propose innovative solutions for sustainability. One such initiative involves the development of a closed-loop system where waste from one part of the production process becomes a resource for another.

0Responsibility and Accountability: The leadership team takes responsibility for the company's environmental impact. They set clear sustainability goals and hold teams accountable for achieving them.

As a result of implementing ZBT with a focus on environmental sustainability:

[111]

The manufacturing company reduces its energy consumption and waste generation, resulting in cost savings and a smaller environmental footprint.

Sustainability initiatives become a source of competitive advantage, attracting environmentally conscious customers and investors.

The company's commitment to environmental responsibility aligns with broader societal expectations and regulations.

This example demonstrates how ZBT's principles, including efficiency, resource optimization, innovation, and responsibility, can drive environmental sustainability efforts within an organization. It highlights the positive impact that a focus on sustainability can have on an organization's environmental footprint and reputation.

Risk Assessment

Zero-Based Thinking's emphasis on risk assessment is a critical component of informed decision-making. It ensures that potential risks are identified, evaluated, and managed systematically, leading to more robust and resilient decision-making processes. By starting from zero and carefully evaluating risks and rewards, organizations can make strategic choices that align with their goals and risk tolerance.

Systematic Evaluation

Systematic evaluation is a crucial aspect of Zero-Based Thinking (ZBT) that encourages a methodical and comprehensive approach to evaluating risks associated with each decision. Instead of relying on assumptions based on past practices, ZBT emphasizes the importance of systematically identifying, analyzing, and assessing potential risks to ensure that no critical factors are overlooked. Here are key aspects to consider:

Comprehensive Risk Assessment: ZBT prompts individuals and organizations to consider a wide range of potential risks associated with a decision, including financial, operational, strategic, and reputational risks.

Risk Identification: It involves systematically identifying all potential risks and uncertainties related to a decision, even those that may not be immediately apparent.

Risk Analysis: ZBT encourages a detailed analysis of each identified risk, including its potential impact, likelihood of occurrence, and any mitigating factors.

Mitigation Strategies: Once risks are identified and analyzed, ZBT guides decision-makers in developing strategies to mitigate or manage these risks effectively.

Informed Decision-Making: The systematic evaluation of risks ensures that decision-makers are well-informed and can make decisions with a clear understanding of the potential consequences and uncertainties involved.

Example

Let's consider how a construction company applies systematic evaluation within a ZBT framework when deciding on a major infrastructure project:

Challenge: The construction company is presented with an opportunity to bid on a large infrastructure project. This project has significant potential for profit but also comes with various risks and uncertainties.

Comprehensive Risk Assessment: The company assembles a cross-functional team to systematically evaluate the project's risks. They consider financial risks, such as cost overruns and fluctuations in materials prices, as well as operational risks related to project execution and potential delays.

Risk Identification: The team identifies a wide range of risks, including adverse weather conditions, permitting delays, supply chain disruptions, labor shortages, and unforeseen geological challenges.

Risk Analysis: Each identified risk is analyzed in detail. For example, they assess the potential impact of adverse weather by reviewing historical weather data for the project location and its potential effect on construction schedules and costs.

Mitigation Strategies: The team develops comprehensive mitigation strategies for each risk. For the risk of supply chain disruptions, they explore alternative suppliers and establish contingency plans. For weather-related risks, they plan for potential schedule adjustments and construction material storage.

Informed Decision-Making: Armed with a thorough understanding of the risks and mitigation strategies, the company's leadership makes an informed decision on whether to bid on the infrastructure project. They weigh the potential profit against the risks and uncertainties and assess whether the project aligns with their risk tolerance and strategic objectives.

As a result of systematic evaluation within the ZBT framework:

[117]

The construction company makes a well-informed decision to bid on the infrastructure project, confident in their ability to manage and mitigate identified risks effectively.

They secure the project, successfully navigate potential challenges, and complete it within the budget and timeline.

The systematic approach to risk evaluation becomes a best practice within the organization, contributing to the successful execution of future projects.

This example illustrates how ZBT's systematic evaluation of risks ensures that organizations make informed decisions, especially in scenarios where significant uncertainties are present. It emphasizes the importance of a structured approach to risk assessment in managing complex projects and decisions effectively.

Identification of Risks

Identification of risks is a foundational aspect of Zero-Based Thinking (ZBT) that emphasizes the importance of starting with a clean slate and proactively identifying potential risks associated with a decision. Decision-makers in a ZBT framework do not assume that a particular decision is inherently safe or risky but instead take deliberate steps to identify and assess various types of risks. These risks may include financial, operational, reputational, or compliance-related risks, among others. Here are key aspects to consider:

Clean Slate Approach: ZBT encourages decision-makers to approach each decision with an open mind, avoiding preconceived notions about its inherent safety or riskiness. This mindset promotes thorough risk assessment.

Proactive Risk Identification: Decision-makers actively seek out and identify potential risks that may arise from a decision. This includes considering both known risks and those that may be less apparent.

Comprehensive Risk Assessment: ZBT prompts a comprehensive evaluation of risks, covering various categories such as financial risks (e.g., budget overruns), operational risks (e.g., process disruptions), reputational risks (e.g., damage to brand image), and compliance risks (e.g., regulatory violations).

Risk Prioritization: After identifying risks, ZBT may involve prioritizing them based on their potential impact and likelihood of occurrence. High-priority risks receive more focused attention and mitigation efforts.

Risk Mitigation Strategies: Decision-makers develop strategies to mitigate or manage identified risks effectively. These strategies are integrated into the decision-making process to minimize potential negative outcomes.

[119]

Example

Let's explore how a pharmaceutical company uses ZBT to identify and assess potential risks when deciding to launch a new drug:

Challenge: The pharmaceutical company is considering the launch of a new drug that has the potential to generate significant revenue but also carries inherent risks.

Clean Slate Approach: The company's decision-makers begin with a clean slate, avoiding any assumptions about the safety or success of launching the new drug. They recognize that even promising drugs can face unforeseen challenges.

Proactive Risk Identification: A cross-functional team, including scientists, marketers, and regulatory experts, is formed to proactively identify potential risks. These risks may include clinical trial setbacks, regulatory hurdles, market competition, adverse side effects, or supply chain disruptions.

Comprehensive Risk Assessment: The team conducts a comprehensive risk assessment, considering various categories of risks. They assess the potential financial impact of clinical trial delays, operational risks associated with scaling up production, reputational risks related to safety concerns, and compliance risks related to regulatory requirements.

Risk Prioritization: After identifying risks, the team prioritizes them based on potential severity and likelihood. Risks with the highest potential impact on patient safety or company finances are identified as top priorities.

Risk Mitigation Strategies: For each high-priority risk, the team develops mitigation strategies. For instance, they implement rigorous quality control measures in production to minimize the risk of defects and adverse side effects. They also plan for alternative regulatory pathways and contingency plans for potential clinical trial delays.

As a result of systematic risk identification within the ZBT framework:

The pharmaceutical company gains a clear understanding of the potential challenges and risks associated with launching the new drug.

They make an informed decision on whether to proceed with the launch, incorporating risk mitigation strategies into their go-to-market plan.

The company's proactive approach to risk identification and mitigation contributes to a successful product launch, minimizing unexpected setbacks and negative outcomes.

This example demonstrates how ZBT's focus on identifying potential risks encourages a proactive and comprehensive approach to decision-making. It underscores the importance of considering various types of risks and developing appropriate mitigation strategies to enhance the likelihood of a successful outcome.

Quantitative and Qualitative Analysis

Quantitative and qualitative analysis are essential components of risk assessment within the framework of Zero-Based Thinking (ZBT). These two approaches work in tandem to provide a comprehensive understanding of risks associated with a decision. Here's an expansion of this concept, along with an illustrative example:

Quantitative Analysis: Quantitative analysis involves assigning numerical values to various aspects of risks, such as probability, potential impact, and financial exposure. This approach allows decision-makers to use data and statistics to assess risks more objectively. Common elements of quantitative analysis in risk assessment include:

Probability Assessment: Assigning probabilities to risks to estimate the likelihood of their occurrence. For example, a 20% probability of a supply chain disruption.

Impact Assessment: Quantifying the potential impact of risks, often in monetary terms. For instance, estimating the financial loss associated with a product recall.

Risk Exposure Calculation: Multiplying the probability and impact values to calculate the overall risk exposure. Higher exposure indicates a risk with greater potential consequences.

Qualitative Analysis: Qualitative analysis complements quantitative assessment by providing a broader understanding of risks. It considers the qualitative aspects of risks, such as the broader context, potential consequences beyond financial impact, and mitigating factors. Key elements of qualitative analysis in risk assessment include:

Contextual Understanding: Assessing risks within the broader context of the organization's goals, values, and strategic objectives. This helps decision-makers consider the relevance and alignment of risks with the organization's mission.

Consequences Beyond Financial Impact: Recognizing that risks can have non-financial consequences, such as reputational damage, legal ramifications, or adverse effects on stakeholders.

Mitigating Factors: Identifying and evaluating the effectiveness of potential risk mitigation strategies and control measures. This involves assessing the organization's preparedness to manage and respond to risks.

Example

Let's explore how a financial institution uses both quantitative and qualitative analysis within a ZBT framework to assess the risk of launching a new financial product:

Challenge: The financial institution is considering the launch of a new financial product aimed at attracting a younger demographic. However, there are potential risks associated with regulatory compliance and reputational damage.

Quantitative Analysis: The institution's risk management team quantitatively assesses the regulatory risk by assigning a probability to regulatory changes impacting the product's compliance. They estimate a 10% probability of regulatory changes within the first year of launch. The potential financial impact, such as fines or penalties, is estimated at $500,000 if regulatory changes occur.

Qualitative Analysis: In parallel, a qualitative analysis considers the broader context and potential consequences. The team identifies that the institution's reputation is at stake, as any regulatory violations could lead to negative media coverage and damage the trust of existing and potential customers.

Mitigating factors include the institution's strong compliance team and its proactive approach to regulatory changes.

By combining both quantitative and qualitative analysis:

The institution gains a comprehensive understanding of the risks associated with launching the new product, including both the numerical probability and potential financial impact of regulatory changes, as well as the broader context and potential non-financial consequences.

Armed with this comprehensive risk assessment, decision-makers can make an informed choice regarding the product launch. They may choose to implement additional safeguards or adjust their strategies to mitigate risks effectively.

This example illustrates how the integration of quantitative and qualitative analysis in risk assessment within the ZBT framework enhances decision-making by providing a more holistic view of potential risks and their implications. It underscores the importance of both numerical data and qualitative insights in understanding the complexity of risks.

Risk Mitigation Strategies

Risk mitigation strategies are a critical component of Zero-Based Thinking (ZBT) that emphasize the importance of developing proactive plans to address and manage identified risks associated with a decision. Once risks are identified and assessed, ZBT requires decision-makers to take deliberate steps to mitigate or manage these risks effectively. These strategies can include alternative approaches, contingency plans, and setting risk tolerance levels. Here's an expansion of this concept, along with an illustrative example:

Alternative Approaches: In some cases, ZBT may involve considering alternative approaches or courses of action that inherently reduce the exposure to specific risks. This approach involves exploring different ways to achieve the same goal while minimizing risk. For example, an organization may choose to source a critical component from multiple suppliers to reduce the risk of supply chain disruptions.

Contingency Plans: ZBT encourages the development of contingency plans that outline predefined actions to be taken in the event that identified risks materialize. These plans are designed to minimize the impact of the risk and enable swift responses. For instance, a contingency plan for a software project may involve a rapid response team to address critical software bugs if they occur.

Risk Tolerance Levels: In some cases, ZBT involves setting clear risk tolerance levels that guide decision-making. Organizations define the acceptable level of risk they are willing to undertake for a particular decision. If the assessed risk exceeds the established tolerance level, it may trigger a reassessment or a decision not to proceed.

Monitoring and Feedback: Risk mitigation strategies often include ongoing monitoring and feedback mechanisms. Decision-makers continually assess the effectiveness of risk mitigation measures and adjust them as necessary. This adaptive approach ensures that strategies remain relevant in the face of changing circumstances.

Example

Let's consider how a construction company applies risk mitigation strategies within a ZBT framework when deciding to undertake a complex infrastructure project:

Challenge: The construction company is evaluating the construction of a bridge in a region prone to severe weather events, such as hurricanes. The project has a high financial potential, but there are significant risks associated with weather-related delays.

Alternative Approaches: In response to the risk of weather-related delays, the company explores alternative construction methods and materials that are more resilient to adverse weather conditions. They also consider scheduling construction during seasons with lower weather risk.

Contingency Plans: The company develops a comprehensive contingency plan that includes a predefined process for assessing weather forecasts and a rapid response team to address potential delays. The plan outlines specific actions to be taken, such as rescheduling work or implementing temporary protective measures if adverse weather is predicted.

Risk Tolerance Levels: The company sets a clear risk tolerance level for the project, specifying the maximum allowable delay and associated cost overrun. If the assessed risk exceeds this tolerance level, the company will reassess the project's feasibility.

Monitoring and Feedback: Throughout the project, the construction company closely monitors weather forecasts and project progress. They use real-time data to assess the effectiveness of their contingency plan and make adjustments as needed to ensure timely completion.

By incorporating these risk mitigation strategies:

The construction company takes a proactive approach to manage the weather-related risks associated with the project.

They are well-prepared to address potential delays swiftly and minimize the project's financial impact.

The risk tolerance level provides clear guidance on when to reassess the project's feasibility if risks escalate.

This example illustrates how ZBT's emphasis on risk mitigation strategies ensures that decision-makers are well-prepared to address potential challenges and uncertainties associated with a decision. It underscores the importance of proactive planning and adaptability in managing risks effectively.

Balancing Risks and Rewards

Balancing risks and rewards is a fundamental aspect of Zero-Based Thinking (ZBT) that guides decision-makers in assessing the potential outcomes of a particular course of action. In the ZBT framework, decision-makers carefully weigh the potential risks associated with a decision against the expected rewards to determine whether the chosen course of action offers a favorable balance. This analysis is critical in making informed and strategic decisions. Here's an expansion of this concept, along with an illustrative example:

Risk Assessment: ZBT begins with a comprehensive risk assessment, where potential risks are identified, analyzed, and prioritized. These risks may encompass financial, operational, reputational, and compliance-related aspects.

Reward Assessment: Decision-makers also evaluate the expected rewards or benefits that can result from the chosen course of action. Rewards may include financial gains, market share expansion, competitive advantages, and strategic alignment.

Risk-Reward Analysis: The heart of the ZBT process involves comparing the potential risks with the anticipated rewards. Decision-makers assess whether the rewards are commensurate with the identified risks and whether the benefits outweigh the potential negative consequences.

Alternative Strategies: ZBT encourages the consideration of alternative strategies or courses of action that may offer a more favorable balance between risks and rewards. This approach ensures that decision-makers explore different options before making a final choice.

Risk Mitigation Strategies: If the analysis reveals that a chosen course of action carries significant risks, ZBT prompts the development of risk mitigation strategies to reduce or manage those risks effectively. These strategies may include contingency plans, alternative approaches, or risk transfer mechanisms.

Example

Let's explore how a technology company applies the principle of balancing risks and rewards within a ZBT framework when deciding to enter a new, highly competitive market:

Challenge: The technology company is considering entering a new market with a product that has the potential to capture a significant share of the market. However, they recognize the market's competitive nature and associated risks.

Risk Assessment: The company conducts a thorough risk assessment, identifying potential risks such as intense competition, market saturation, regulatory challenges, and uncertain consumer adoption.

Reward Assessment: Simultaneously, they evaluate the potential rewards, including revenue projections, market expansion, diversification, and strategic positioning.

Risk-Reward Analysis: Decision-makers analyze the identified risks and compare them to the expected rewards. They recognize that the market's competitiveness poses substantial risks but also acknowledge the substantial rewards if successful.

Alternative Strategies: In light of the high risks, the company explores alternative strategies, such as entering adjacent markets or diversifying product offerings. They assess the balance of risks and rewards for each option.

Risk Mitigation Strategies: The company develops risk mitigation strategies, including a robust marketing plan, competitive pricing strategies, and a contingency plan in case initial market penetration is slower than expected.

By incorporating this risk-reward analysis:

The technology company gains a clear understanding of the trade-offs between the potential risks and rewards associated with entering the new market.

They make an informed decision on whether to proceed, considering both the competitive challenges and the potential for significant market share.

This example illustrates how ZBT's emphasis on balancing risks and rewards ensures that decision-makers carefully consider the implications of their choices. It underscores the importance of making strategic decisions that align with an organization's risk tolerance and long-term objectives.

Decision Quality

Decision quality is a critical outcome of Zero-Based Thinking (ZBT), driven by the rigorous risk assessment and evaluation processes within the framework. ZBT ensures that decisions are made with a high level of scrutiny and understanding, leading to improved decision quality. Here's an expansion of this concept, along with an illustrative example:

Risk Assessment: ZBT begins with a comprehensive risk assessment, which involves identifying, analyzing, and prioritizing potential risks associated with a decision. This thorough examination ensures that all potential challenges and uncertainties are considered.

Data-Driven Analysis: Decision-makers in a ZBT framework rely on data, evidence, and objective analysis when assessing risks and rewards. Quantitative and qualitative data support informed decision-making.

Risk Mitigation Strategies: ZBT requires the development of risk mitigation strategies. These strategies are designed to address identified risks and minimize their potential impact on the decision's outcome.

Balancing Risks and Rewards: Decision-makers perform a risk-reward analysis, carefully weighing the potential risks against the expected rewards. This analysis helps determine whether the chosen course of action aligns with the organization's risk tolerance and strategic objectives.

Alternative Consideration: ZBT encourages the exploration of alternative strategies or options, ensuring that decision-makers consider a range of possibilities before making a final choice.

Continuous Improvement: ZBT is an iterative process that supports continuous improvement. Decision-makers monitor the outcomes of their decisions and adjust their strategies as needed based on real-world results.

Example

Let's examine how a healthcare organization uses ZBT to improve the quality of its decisions when considering the implementation of a new electronic health record (EHR) system:

Challenge: The healthcare organization recognizes the need to upgrade its EHR system to improve patient care and streamline operations. However, the implementation of a new EHR system poses significant risks, including potential disruptions to patient care, data security concerns, and financial costs.

Risk Assessment: The organization conducts a comprehensive risk assessment, identifying potential risks such as data migration challenges, staff training requirements, and the potential for operational disruptions during the transition.

Data-Driven Analysis: Decision-makers gather data on EHR system options, considering factors such as vendor track record, system functionality, and costs. They rely on historical data to assess the potential for data migration challenges and operational disruptions.

Risk Mitigation Strategies: To address identified risks, the organization develops a detailed implementation plan that includes staff training programs, data backup strategies, and contingency plans for potential disruptions to patient care.

Balancing Risks and Rewards: Decision-makers perform a risk-reward analysis, weighing the potential risks (e.g., implementation challenges) against the expected rewards (e.g., improved patient care and operational efficiency). They ensure that the decision aligns with the organization's mission and risk tolerance.

Alternative Consideration: As part of the ZBT process, the organization explores alternative EHR system options and implementation strategies, comparing them to the primary choice to ensure they select the most suitable option.

Continuous Improvement: After implementing the new EHR system, the organization continually monitors its performance, collects feedback from staff and patients, and makes adjustments to further enhance its effectiveness.

By applying ZBT in this scenario:

The healthcare organization makes an informed decision about the new EHR system, understanding the potential risks and benefits fully.

The organization's decision-making process is characterized by thorough analysis and mitigation of identified risks, leading to higher decision quality.

Continuous improvement efforts ensure that the EHR system's implementation aligns with the organization's strategic objectives and contributes to improved patient care.

This example illustrates how ZBT's commitment to rigorous risk assessment and decision analysis enhances the quality of decisions, especially in complex and high-stakes situations. It underscores the importance of informed, data-driven decision-making that aligns with an organization's mission and objectives.

Risk Communication

Risk communication is a crucial element of Zero-Based Thinking (ZBT) that promotes open and transparent sharing of risk-related information within an organization. When decision-makers rigorously assess and document risks, it becomes easier to communicate these risks effectively to relevant stakeholders. This practice fosters a culture of transparency, accountability, and informed decision-making. Here's an expansion of this concept, along with an illustrative example:

Thorough Risk Assessment: ZBT begins with a comprehensive risk assessment process where potential risks are identified, analyzed, and prioritized. This process involves evaluating both quantitative and qualitative aspects of risks.

Documentation of Risks: Decision-makers document identified risks along with their probability, potential impact, and relevant mitigation strategies. This documentation serves as a foundation for clear and organized risk communication.

Stakeholder Involvement: ZBT encourages involving relevant stakeholders in the risk assessment and communication process. This ensures that diverse perspectives are considered and that those who will be affected by the decision are informed.

Transparency: Decision-makers are encouraged to be transparent about the identified risks, sharing them openly with stakeholders, including senior leadership, board members, employees, and even external partners when necessary.

Accountability: Transparent risk communication promotes accountability. When risks are communicated clearly, it is easier to attribute responsibility for risk management and mitigation efforts.

Informed Decision-Making: Clear risk communication helps decision-makers and stakeholders make informed choices by providing a full understanding of the potential challenges and uncertainties associated with a decision.

Example

Let's explore how a manufacturing company applies risk communication within a ZBT framework when deciding to launch a new product line:

Challenge: The manufacturing company is considering the introduction of a new product line in a highly competitive market. The decision involves financial risks, market saturation risks, and operational risks related to production capacity.

Thorough Risk Assessment: The company conducts a comprehensive risk assessment, identifying potential risks such as market demand fluctuations, production bottlenecks, and increased competition.

Documentation of Risks: The risks identified are documented in a clear and organized manner, including probability estimates and potential financial impacts. This documentation includes risk mitigation strategies, such as plans for optimizing production efficiency.

Stakeholder Involvement: Relevant stakeholders, including the executive team, production managers, and sales teams, are involved in the risk assessment process to provide their insights and perspectives on potential risks.

Transparency: The results of the risk assessment are communicated transparently to the company's leadership and employees. A risk summary document is shared, highlighting the key risks, their potential impacts, and the proposed mitigation strategies.

Accountability: By sharing the risk assessment openly, accountability for managing and mitigating these risks is clearly assigned to specific teams and individuals within the organization.

Informed Decision-Making: Armed with a thorough understanding of the potential risks and rewards, decision-makers make an informed choice on whether to proceed with the new product line. This decision is made with the full knowledge of the associated challenges.

By incorporating risk communication in this manner:

The manufacturing company ensures that all relevant stakeholders are informed about the potential risks and rewards of the new product line, fostering transparency and accountability.

Decision-makers have access to a clear risk assessment document that guides their choices and supports informed decision-making.

The company is better prepared to address identified risks and implement effective mitigation strategies.

This example demonstrates how ZBT's emphasis on risk communication promotes transparency and accountability within the organization. It highlights the importance of sharing risk-related information openly to facilitate informed decision-making and effective risk management.

Adaptive Decision-Making

Adaptive decision-making is a fundamental aspect of Zero-Based Thinking (ZBT) that recognizes the dynamic nature of risks and circumstances. ZBT encourages organizations to periodically revisit their risk assessments, strategies, and decisions, allowing them to adjust and adapt in response to changing conditions. This adaptability is crucial for effectively managing evolving risks and ensuring that decisions remain aligned with organizational goals. Here's an expansion of this concept, along with an illustrative example:

Initial Risk Assessment: ZBT begins with an initial risk assessment during the decision-making process, where potential risks are identified, analyzed, and prioritized. Strategies and mitigation plans are developed based on this assessment.

Regular Reviews: ZBT promotes the practice of regular reviews and reassessments of the identified risks and the effectiveness of risk mitigation strategies. This may involve periodic check-ins, scheduled assessments, or real-time monitoring of key risk indicators.

Data-Driven Analysis: Decision-makers rely on data, evidence, and feedback when revisiting risk assessments. They gather information about changing market conditions, emerging threats, or shifts in internal capabilities that may impact the organization's risk landscape.

Adjustment of Strategies: Based on the findings of the reviews and reassessments, organizations are encouraged to adjust their strategies as necessary. This may involve updating risk mitigation plans, reallocating resources, or exploring alternative courses of action.

Communication: The results of these periodic reviews are communicated transparently within the organization to relevant stakeholders. This fosters a culture of adaptability and ensures that all decision-makers are aware of evolving risks.

Example

Let's consider how a technology company practices adaptive decision-making within a ZBT framework when managing cybersecurity risks:

Challenge: The technology company has implemented a comprehensive cybersecurity strategy to protect its systems and data. However, the cybersecurity landscape is constantly evolving, with new threats and vulnerabilities emerging regularly.

Initial Risk Assessment: The company conducts an initial risk assessment to identify potential cybersecurity risks, including data breaches, malware attacks, and social engineering threats. A robust cybersecurity strategy is developed based on this assessment.

Regular Reviews: Recognizing the dynamic nature of cybersecurity threats, the company establishes a regular review schedule. Every quarter, the cybersecurity team conducts a comprehensive reassessment of existing risks and threats.

Data-Driven Analysis: During these quarterly reviews, the team collects data on the latest cybersecurity threats, industry trends, and the effectiveness of current security measures. They also monitor the organization's historical data on security incidents.

Adjustment of Strategies: Based on the findings of the reviews, the company adjusts its cybersecurity strategies and mitigation plans. This may involve updating firewall rules, enhancing employee training, or investing in advanced threat detection tools.

Communication: The results of the quarterly reviews are communicated to senior leadership, IT teams, and employees involved in cybersecurity. This ensures that everyone is aware of the evolving threat landscape and any changes to the organization's security measures.

By incorporating adaptive decision-making in this manner:

The technology company remains agile in responding to changing cybersecurity threats and vulnerabilities.

Decision-makers have access to up-to-date information when adjusting their strategies, which enhances the effectiveness of their risk mitigation efforts.

The organization fosters a culture of adaptability and continuous improvement in cybersecurity.

This example illustrates how ZBT's emphasis on adaptive decision-making ensures that organizations can respond proactively to evolving risks and circumstances. It highlights the importance of regular reviews and adjustments to maintain the relevance and effectiveness of risk management strategies.

Compliance and Regulatory Considerations

Compliance and regulatory considerations play a critical role in risk management, especially in industries where adherence to laws and standards is essential. Zero-Based Thinking (ZBT) incorporates compliance and regulatory aspects into its risk assessment process, ensuring that organizations proactively identify and mitigate risks associated with non-compliance. Here's an expansion of this concept, along with an illustrative example:

Incorporation of Compliance Factors: ZBT's risk assessment process involves considering compliance requirements and regulatory standards from the outset. This ensures that compliance-related risks are integrated into the overall risk assessment framework.

Identification of Compliance Risks: During the risk assessment, organizations identify potential compliance risks, which may include failing to meet industry-specific regulations, data privacy laws, environmental standards, or occupational safety regulations. These risks are evaluated in terms of their potential impact and likelihood.

Documentation of Compliance Measures: As part of the risk assessment, organizations document the measures in place to address compliance requirements. This includes policies, procedures, training programs, and audit processes designed to ensure adherence to relevant regulations.

Periodic Compliance Reviews: ZBT promotes the practice of regular compliance reviews to assess the effectiveness of existing measures and identify any gaps or emerging compliance risks. These reviews are conducted in alignment with industry-specific compliance cycles and requirements.

Adjustment of Compliance Strategies: Based on the findings of compliance reviews and changes in regulations, organizations

[140]

adjust their compliance strategies and measures as necessary. This may involve updating policies, enhancing employee training, or implementing new technologies to support compliance efforts.

Communication of Compliance Status: The compliance status and any changes or improvements are communicated transparently within the organization. This ensures that relevant stakeholders are aware of compliance-related risks and the organization's efforts to mitigate them.

Example

Let's explore how a pharmaceutical company incorporates compliance and regulatory considerations within a ZBT framework when developing and launching a new drug:

Challenge: The pharmaceutical company is preparing to launch a new drug in a highly regulated industry. Compliance with various regulations, including FDA guidelines, is crucial to ensure patient safety, product efficacy, and legal adherence.

Incorporation of Compliance Factors: From the outset of the drug development process, ZBT ensures that compliance with FDA regulations and other relevant industry standards is considered a fundamental part of the risk assessment process.

Identification of Compliance Risks: The company identifies compliance-related risks, such as potential deviations from FDA guidelines during drug development, data integrity issues, or insufficient documentation of clinical trials.

Documentation of Compliance Measures: Throughout the drug development process, the company documents its compliance measures, which include adherence to FDA guidance on clinical trial conduct, data integrity protocols, and quality assurance practices.

Periodic Compliance Reviews: In alignment with regulatory requirements, the company conducts regular compliance reviews and audits of its clinical trial data, documentation, and manufacturing processes. These reviews ensure that compliance measures are effective and up to date.

Adjustment of Compliance Strategies: Based on the findings of compliance reviews and changes in FDA regulations, the company adjusts its compliance strategies. For example, it may update its data management systems to enhance data integrity or refine its manufacturing processes to meet new quality standards.

Communication of Compliance Status: The results of compliance reviews and any changes to compliance strategies are communicated transparently within the organization. This includes sharing compliance reports with regulatory affairs teams, quality control teams, and senior leadership.

By incorporating compliance and regulatory considerations in this manner:

The pharmaceutical company ensures that it meets all regulatory requirements for drug development and launch, minimizing the risk of non-compliance.

Decision-makers have access to a comprehensive understanding of compliance-related risks and measures, supporting informed decision-making.

The organization fosters a culture of compliance and accountability throughout its operations.

This example demonstrates how ZBT's inclusion of compliance and regulatory considerations helps organizations effectively manage compliance-related risks and maintain legal adherence in regulated industries. It underscores the importance of proactive compliance efforts and regular reviews to adapt to evolving regulations.

Innovation and Risk

Innovation and risk are intertwined, and Zero-Based Thinking (ZBT) recognizes that calculated risk-taking can be a driver of innovation. ZBT encourages organizations to carefully assess the potential risks and rewards of innovative ideas, allowing them to make informed decisions that strike a balance between the imperative for innovation and prudent risk management. Here's an expansion of this concept, along with an illustrative example:

Risk Assessment for Innovation: ZBT's risk assessment process encompasses innovative initiatives. Organizations actively identify and evaluate potential risks associated with innovative projects, such as financial investments, market uncertainties, technological challenges, and regulatory compliance.

Balancing Risk and Reward: Decision-makers employ a risk-reward analysis to assess whether the potential benefits of innovation outweigh the identified risks. This analysis guides the determination of whether an innovative project is worth pursuing.

Innovation Strategy: ZBT encourages organizations to align their innovation strategy with their broader goals and risk tolerance. This ensures that innovation efforts are consistent with the organization's mission and objectives.

Mitigating Innovation Risks: While embracing innovation, ZBT also involves developing risk mitigation strategies specific to innovative projects. These strategies may include contingency plans, technology partnerships, or phased project approaches to reduce potential risks.

Transparency in Decision-Making: ZBT fosters transparent communication about the risks and rewards of innovative endeavors within the organization. This ensures that all stakeholders are aware of the calculated risks associated with innovation.

Example

Let's explore how a technology startup uses ZBT to assess the risks and rewards of developing a groundbreaking new product:

Challenge: The startup is considering developing a new, cutting-edge product that leverages emerging technologies. While the potential rewards are substantial, there are significant risks, including technical challenges, market competition, and a substantial upfront investment.

Risk Assessment for Innovation: Within a ZBT framework, the startup conducts a comprehensive risk assessment of the innovative project. They identify potential risks, such as technological uncertainties, intellectual property challenges, and market adoption hurdles.

Balancing Risk and Reward: Decision-makers perform a thorough risk-reward analysis, considering the potential benefits of launching the innovative product, such as market leadership and revenue growth, alongside the identified risks.

Innovation Strategy: The startup aligns its innovation strategy with its overall business goals. They ensure that the innovative product aligns with their mission to disrupt the market and provide unique value.

Mitigating Innovation Risks: To mitigate risks, the startup invests in technology partnerships with leading experts in the field, conducts rigorous testing and quality assurance, and develops a phased product launch plan to minimize market entry risks.

Transparency in Decision-Making: The risk assessment and innovation strategy are communicated transparently to the startup's team, investors, and key stakeholders. This open communication ensures that everyone is aware of the calculated risks associated with the innovative product development.

By incorporating ZBT into their innovation process:

The startup makes an informed decision to pursue the innovative product, understanding both its potential benefits and the risks involved.

Decision-makers have a clear understanding of the calculated risks and are prepared with mitigation strategies.

The organization fosters a culture of innovation while maintaining a prudent approach to risk management.

This example demonstrates how ZBT encourages organizations to embrace innovation as a calculated risk, ensuring that they make informed decisions that align with their strategic goals and risk tolerance. It highlights the importance of balancing risk and reward in innovation endeavors and communicating transparently about these risks within the organization.

Zero-Based Thinking for Business

In business, Zero-Based Thinking promotes a mindset of continuous improvement, innovation, and efficiency. By challenging established practices and starting from zero, individuals and organizations can uncover new opportunities, make informed decisions, and adapt to changing circumstances more effectively. This flexibility and adaptability are essential in today's rapidly evolving world.

Cost Management

Cost management is a critical application of Zero-Based Thinking (ZBT) that enables organizations to optimize their expenses by scrutinizing and justifying every cost. This approach is particularly valuable during challenging economic times or when organizations need to make the most of their budgets. Here's an expansion of this concept, along with an illustrative example:

Comprehensive Expense Review: ZBT begins with a comprehensive review of all expenses, requiring organizations to evaluate each line item individually. This review covers everything from operational costs to discretionary spending.

No Assumptions: Under ZBT, no expense is assumed to be necessary by default. Decision-makers must provide a compelling reason for each expenditure, starting from a clean slate.

Resource Allocation: ZBT prompts organizations to align their resources with strategic priorities, ensuring that expenses contribute directly to achieving business objectives.

Identification of Waste: By scrutinizing every cost, organizations can identify areas of inefficiency, waste, or redundancy. This allows for targeted cost-cutting efforts.

Budget Realignment: ZBT often results in the reallocation of resources to areas that have a higher strategic impact. This ensures that resources are directed toward activities that drive the most value.

Regular Reviews: ZBT is not a one-time exercise; it's an ongoing process. Organizations continually reassess their expenses, adjusting them as conditions change and new information becomes available.

Example

Let's explore how a retail chain uses ZBT to streamline store operations and manage costs more effectively:

Challenge: The retail chain operates numerous stores, and each store has its own set of operational expenses. The company wants to optimize store operations and reduce unnecessary costs.

Comprehensive Expense Review: Within a ZBT framework, the retail chain conducts a thorough review of all store expenses, including rent, utilities, staffing, inventory management, and marketing.

No Assumptions: The review starts with no assumptions. Each expense is evaluated individually, and decision-makers must provide a justification for its necessity.

Resource Allocation: The retail chain aligns its resources with strategic priorities. For example, it reallocates marketing funds to focus on more profitable customer segments and reduces excess inventory levels.

Identification of Waste: Through the ZBT process, the company identifies areas of waste, such as overstaffing during non-peak hours or excess inventory that ties up capital unnecessarily.

Budget Realignment: As a result of the ZBT exercise, the retail chain reallocates resources to stores in high-growth markets, ensuring that funds are directed toward locations with the most significant potential for revenue generation.

Regular Reviews: The retail chain incorporates ZBT into its ongoing operations. Store expenses are periodically reviewed and adjusted based on changing market conditions and performance metrics.

By incorporating ZBT into their cost management approach:

[151]

The retail chain identifies and eliminates unnecessary costs, leading to more efficient store operations.

Decision-makers have a clear understanding of why each expense is necessary, and resources are directed to where they can have the most impact.

The organization fosters a culture of continuous cost optimization and resource allocation based on strategic priorities.

This example demonstrates how ZBT's emphasis on reviewing and justifying expenses can help organizations optimize their budgets and streamline operations. It highlights the value of regular reviews and aligning expenses with strategic goals to ensure cost-effectiveness and efficiency.

Budgeting

Budgeting is a fundamental area where Zero-Based Thinking (ZBT) can have a transformative impact, turning the budgeting process from a routine task into a strategic endeavor. ZBT requires organizations to thoroughly evaluate and justify every expenditure, focusing on alignment with strategic goals and current needs. This approach ensures that budgets are tailored to the organization's evolving priorities. Here's an expansion of this concept, along with an illustrative example:

Shift from Routine to Strategic: ZBT challenges the traditional approach to budgeting, which often involves adjusting the previous year's budget with minor changes. Instead, it promotes a strategic mindset, where each expenditure is considered in the context of the organization's current goals and objectives.

Justification of Every Expense: Under ZBT, no expense is assumed to be necessary by default. Budget owners and decision-makers must provide a compelling reason for each expenditure, starting from a blank slate.

Alignment with Strategic Goals: The core principle of ZBT is aligning resources with strategic priorities. Budgets are built around what's needed to achieve specific objectives, ensuring that every dollar spent contributes directly to the organization's mission.

Resource Optimization: By challenging the necessity of each expense, organizations can identify areas where resources can be optimized, reallocated, or repurposed for maximum impact.

Dynamic Budgeting: ZBT promotes dynamic budgeting, where budgets are adjusted and realigned as circumstances change. This flexibility allows organizations to respond to shifting priorities and market conditions.

[153]

Continuous Improvement: Budgeting under ZBT is not a one-time exercise; it's an ongoing process. Organizations continually reassess their budgets to ensure that they remain aligned with their strategic goals.

Example

Let's consider how a technology company applies ZBT to its annual budgeting process:

Challenge: The technology company operates in a fast-paced industry, and its strategic priorities evolve rapidly. It wants to ensure that its budget aligns with its ever-changing goals.

Shift from Routine to Strategic: Instead of rolling over the previous year's budget with minor adjustments, the company embraces ZBT for its budgeting process, recognizing that it requires a more strategic approach.

Justification of Every Expense: The budgeting team, in collaboration with department heads, evaluates every expenditure. They ask critical questions such as, "How does this expense contribute to our current strategic initiatives?" and "Is there a more efficient way to achieve this goal?"

Alignment with Strategic Goals: The budget is built around the company's current strategic goals, which include expanding into new markets and investing in research and development to drive innovation.

Resource Optimization: Through the ZBT process, the company identifies areas where resources can be optimized. For instance, they streamline marketing expenses by focusing on digital channels that provide better ROI.

Dynamic Budgeting: The ZBT approach enables the company to make budget adjustments throughout the year in response to changing market dynamics and emerging opportunities.

Continuous Improvement: The company incorporates ZBT principles into its budgeting culture, ensuring that budgets are regularly reviewed and adjusted to maintain alignment with strategic priorities.

By incorporating ZBT into their budgeting process:

The technology company ensures that its budget is closely aligned with its strategic goals, allowing for more effective resource allocation.

Decision-makers have a clear understanding of why each expenditure is necessary and how it contributes to the company's mission.

The organization fosters a culture of continuous improvement and adaptability in budgeting.

This example demonstrates how ZBT's emphasis on strategic thinking and justification of expenses can enhance the budgeting process, ensuring that budgets are dynamic, aligned with organizational goals, and optimized for current needs.

Resource Allocation

Resource allocation is a critical aspect of organizational management, and Zero-Based Thinking (ZBT) provides a systematic approach to optimize the allocation of resources according to strategic objectives. ZBT emphasizes that resources, including personnel, capital, and time, should be directed toward activities that generate the most value and enhance overall efficiency. This approach enables organizations to respond more flexibly to changing market conditions. Here's an expansion of this concept, along with an illustrative example:

Strategic Resource Allocation: ZBT starts by aligning resource allocation with an organization's strategic objectives. It ensures that every resource expenditure serves a clear purpose in advancing the organization's mission.

Justification of Resource Use: Under ZBT, every resource allocation is justified based on its value contribution. This requires a thorough evaluation of the necessity and efficiency of each resource deployment.

Optimizing Resource Mix: ZBT encourages organizations to assess the mix of resources they allocate, balancing personnel, financial capital, technology, and time investments to maximize their collective impact.

Flexible Response to Change: By regularly reevaluating resource allocation decisions, ZBT allows organizations to respond quickly to changing market conditions, emerging opportunities, and evolving strategic priorities.

Continuous Improvement: ZBT fosters a culture of continuous improvement in resource allocation, ensuring that organizations regularly reassess and optimize their resource allocation strategies.

Example

Let's explore how a startup technology company uses ZBT to allocate its resources effectively:

Challenge: The startup operates in a highly competitive tech sector and wants to ensure that it allocates its limited resources strategically to achieve rapid growth and product development.

Strategic Resource Allocation: The company adopts ZBT principles to align resource allocation with its strategic objectives, which include gaining market share, launching new products, and expanding into new geographic regions.

Justification of Resource Use: Under ZBT, the leadership team thoroughly evaluates each resource allocation decision. For instance, they assess whether hiring additional engineers is necessary to accelerate product development or if it would be more cost-effective to form strategic partnerships.

Optimizing Resource Mix: The company optimizes its resource mix by reallocating capital from non-essential areas to fund critical research and development projects. Additionally, they allocate human resources to key growth initiatives, ensuring that the right talent is assigned to high-impact projects.

Flexible Response to Change: ZBT enables the startup to respond flexibly to market shifts. For example, when they identify emerging trends in a new market segment, they swiftly reallocate resources to capitalize on the opportunity, reallocating funds from less promising initiatives.

Continuous Improvement: The startup embeds ZBT principles into its resource allocation culture, conducting regular assessments and making adjustments to ensure that resources are optimally aligned with strategic objectives.

By incorporating ZBT into their resource allocation process:

The startup ensures that resources are directed to the most critical activities that drive growth and innovation.

Decision-makers have a clear understanding of how each resource allocation decision contributes to the company's strategic goals.

The organization fosters a culture of adaptability and continuous improvement in resource allocation.

This example illustrates how ZBT's emphasis on strategic resource allocation and ongoing optimization enables organizations to make efficient use of their resources and respond effectively to changing market dynamics.

Project Management

Project management is a field where Zero-Based Thinking (ZBT) can be highly beneficial. ZBT encourages project teams to regularly reevaluate project plans and budgets, ensuring that they align with project objectives and strategic goals. This proactive approach helps identify potential scope creep, inefficiencies, and risks, allowing for timely adjustments and improved project outcomes. Here's an expansion of this concept, along with an illustrative example:

Regular Project Reevaluation: ZBT promotes the idea that project management is not a static process but rather a dynamic one that requires periodic reassessment. Project teams should regularly review project plans, budgets, and timelines.

Identification of Scope Creep: ZBT helps project teams recognize scope creep, which occurs when additional work or features are introduced into the project without proper evaluation. By scrutinizing changes against the project's original scope, ZBT helps prevent unnecessary expansions.

Efficiency Assessment: ZBT encourages project teams to assess the efficiency of their processes and resource utilization. This includes evaluating whether there are more cost-effective ways to complete tasks and deliverables.

Risk Management: The regular review process under ZBT includes a thorough assessment of project risks. By identifying potential risks early, teams can develop mitigation strategies to avoid or minimize their impact.

Timely Adjustments: ZBT emphasizes the importance of making timely adjustments to project plans and budgets based on the results of regular reevaluations. This ensures that projects stay on track and within budget.

Improved Outcomes: By proactively addressing scope creep, inefficiencies, and risks, ZBT contributes to improved project outcomes, including on-time delivery, budget adherence, and successful achievement of project goals.

Example

Let's consider how a construction project uses ZBT in project management to ensure efficiency and mitigate potential issues:

Challenge: A construction company is tasked with building a new office complex for a client. The project has a strict budget and timeline, and any delays or cost overruns would be detrimental to both parties.

Regular Project Reevaluation: The project management team adopts ZBT principles and schedules regular reviews of the project plan and budget at predefined intervals.

Identification of Scope Creep: During one of the project reviews, the team identifies potential scope creep. The client has requested additional features, such as a rooftop garden, that were not part of the original project scope.

[159]

Efficiency Assessment: Through the ZBT process, the team evaluates construction processes and identifies areas where efficiency can be improved. They find that using prefabricated materials for certain components can save time and reduce costs.

Risk Management: The project team conducts a risk assessment and identifies the risk of unfavorable weather conditions affecting the construction schedule. They develop contingency plans, such as rescheduling activities during favorable weather windows.

Timely Adjustments: Based on the results of their assessments, the project team makes timely adjustments to the project plan. They negotiate with the client to manage scope changes effectively and incorporate efficiency improvements into the construction process.

Improved Outcomes: By incorporating ZBT principles into their project management approach, the construction project is completed within the specified timeline and budget. The project achieves its goals and satisfies the client's additional requests without compromising efficiency.

By incorporating ZBT into their project management practices:

The construction project team proactively manages scope changes and identifies areas for efficiency improvements.

Decision-makers have a clear understanding of how each adjustment contributes to successful project outcomes.

The organization fosters a culture of adaptability and continuous improvement in project management.

This example demonstrates how ZBT's focus on regular reevaluation and proactive adjustments can enhance project management processes, leading to more efficient project delivery and improved outcomes.

Product Development

Product development is a crucial area where Zero-Based Thinking (ZBT) can drive innovation and efficiency. ZBT encourages teams to challenge assumptions and established practices in the design and manufacturing processes. This approach can lead to more innovative products and streamlined production, ultimately reducing costs and enhancing competitiveness. Here's an expansion of this concept, along with an illustrative example:

Questioning Assumptions: ZBT encourages product development teams to question assumptions about product features, design principles, and manufacturing methods. Rather than following established norms, teams start with a clean slate.

Innovative Product Design: ZBT promotes innovative thinking in product design. Teams are encouraged to explore unconventional ideas and consider how products can be redesigned to better meet customer needs or offer unique features.

Efficiency in Manufacturing: By challenging manufacturing processes, ZBT can lead to more efficient and cost-effective production methods. This includes evaluating the use of materials, automation, and supply chain logistics.

Cost Reduction: ZBT helps identify opportunities for cost reduction by eliminating unnecessary features or processes. This is essential for maintaining competitiveness in markets with price-sensitive customers.

Competitive Advantage: The outcome of ZBT-driven product development is often a product that stands out in the market due to its innovation, cost-effectiveness, or unique features. This competitive advantage can lead to increased market share.

Customer-Centric Approach: ZBT encourages a customer-centric approach, where product development decisions are based on a deep understanding of customer needs and preferences.

Example

Let's consider how an electronics company applies ZBT to the development of a new smartphone:

Challenge: The company wants to create a smartphone that not only competes in terms of features but also stands out with a unique selling proposition.

Questioning Assumptions: The product development team begins by questioning assumptions about what a smartphone should look like and what features it must have. Instead of following the industry standard, they start with a blank canvas.

Innovative Product Design: Through ZBT, the team explores unconventional design ideas. They consider factors like ergonomic improvements, novel user interfaces, and the integration of emerging technologies like augmented reality.

Efficiency in Manufacturing: ZBT leads the team to evaluate manufacturing processes. They identify opportunities to reduce material waste, optimize assembly procedures, and consider automated quality control measures.

Cost Reduction: The team identifies features that are seldom used by customers and decides to remove them to reduce production costs. They also explore alternative materials that are both durable and cost-effective.

Competitive Advantage: By delivering a smartphone with a unique user experience and competitive pricing, the company gains a significant advantage in the market.

Customer-Centric Approach: ZBT ensures that the final product is designed with a deep understanding of customer preferences, resulting in a smartphone that addresses pain points and provides a superior user experience.

By incorporating ZBT into their product development process:

The electronics company fosters a culture of innovation and unconventional thinking, resulting in a smartphone that stands out in the market.

Decision-makers have a clear understanding of how each design and manufacturing decision contributes to the product's competitiveness.

The organization prioritizes customer needs, ultimately delivering a product that resonates with the target audience.

This example demonstrates how ZBT's emphasis on questioning assumptions and seeking innovative solutions can lead to the development of products that are not only competitive but also differentiated in the market. It highlights the importance of cost-efficiency and a customer-centric approach in product development.

Zero-Based Thinking for Personal Success

For an individual, Zero-Based Thinking promotes a mindset of continuous improvement, innovation, and efficiency. By challenging your established habits and ways of doing things, and starting from zero, individuals and organizations can uncover new opportunities, make informed decisions, and adapt to changing circumstances more effectively. This flexibility and adaptability are essential in today's rapidly evolving world.

Financial Planning

Financial planning is a personal area where Zero-Based Thinking (ZBT) can help individuals take control of their finances, identify savings opportunities, and allocate resources more effectively toward their financial goals. ZBT principles encourage individuals to review their expenses, create budgets from scratch, and justify every expenditure. Here's an expansion of this concept, along with an illustrative example:

Expense Review: ZBT starts with a thorough review of all expenses, both fixed and variable. This involves questioning the necessity and value of each expense, from utility bills to subscription services.

Budgeting from Scratch: Instead of starting with an existing budget, ZBT requires individuals to create a budget from scratch. This process allows for a fresh perspective on how income should be allocated.

Justification of Expenditures: Under ZBT, individuals must justify every expenditure based on its alignment with their financial goals. This encourages a deliberate approach to spending.

Identification of Savings Opportunities: By scrutinizing expenses, ZBT helps individuals identify areas where savings can be realized, such as reducing discretionary spending or finding more cost-effective alternatives.

Resource Allocation: ZBT promotes the allocation of financial resources to meet specific financial goals, whether it's building an emergency fund, saving for retirement, or paying off debt.

Debt Reduction: Individuals can use ZBT to assess their debt obligations and create a plan for paying down debts efficiently, thus saving on interest payments.

[168]

Example

Let's consider how an individual applies ZBT to their personal financial planning:

Challenge: The individual is seeking to improve their financial health, increase savings, and reduce unnecessary expenses.

Expense Review: The individual conducts a thorough review of their expenses, including rent or mortgage, utilities, groceries, transportation, entertainment, and subscriptions.

Budgeting from Scratch: Instead of relying on their existing budget, they create a new budget from scratch, starting with their monthly income.

Justification of Expenditures: For each expense category, the individual justifies the necessity of the expense. For example, they evaluate whether a premium cable TV package is providing enough value to justify the cost.

Identification of Savings Opportunities: During the review, they identify areas where they can save money. They realize that by canceling unused subscriptions and switching to a more cost-effective cell phone plan, they can reduce their monthly expenses.

Resource Allocation: With a clearer view of their financial situation, they allocate a portion of their income to an emergency fund and retirement savings. This ensures that their financial goals are prioritized in their budget.

Debt Reduction: If the individual has outstanding credit card debt, they develop a plan to pay it down systematically. They allocate a portion of their budget specifically for debt repayment.

By incorporating ZBT principles into their financial planning:

[169]

The individual gains a clearer understanding of their financial situation and priorities.

Decision-making is more intentional, with each expenditure aligned with specific financial goals.

The individual can identify and realize savings opportunities, reduce debt, and allocate resources more effectively toward savings and investments.

This example illustrates how ZBT's emphasis on reviewing expenses, budgeting from scratch, and justifying expenditures can empower individuals to take control of their finances and work toward achieving their financial goals.

Goal Setting

Goal setting is a personal development area where Zero-Based Thinking (ZBT) can be a powerful approach. ZBT encourages individuals to set and achieve their personal goals by avoiding assumptions and starting from a clean slate. It involves evaluating new approaches and methods to reach objectives, which can lead to more creative and efficient pathways to success. Here's an expansion of this concept, along with an illustrative example:

Assumption Avoidance: ZBT begins by avoiding assumptions that past strategies will work in the future. Individuals should question whether their current approaches are still effective and relevant.

Starting from Zero: Instead of continuing with established methods, individuals should start from a clean slate when setting new goals. This allows for a fresh perspective on how to achieve objectives.

Innovative Goal Setting: ZBT encourages innovative goal setting. It involves exploring unconventional or unique ways to achieve desired outcomes and considering different strategies and approaches.

Efficiency and Effectiveness: By evaluating new approaches, individuals can identify more efficient and effective ways to reach their goals. This may involve using new technologies, seeking expert guidance, or adopting novel methods.

Continuous Improvement: ZBT promotes an ongoing process of evaluation and adjustment in pursuit of personal goals. It encourages individuals to regularly assess their progress and make necessary changes to stay on course.

Example

Let's consider how an individual applies ZBT to set and achieve a personal goal, such as improving physical fitness:

Challenge: The individual aims to improve their physical fitness and overall health but has struggled to see progress using their current exercise routine.

Assumption Avoidance: The individual realizes that they have been assuming their current exercise routine is effective. However, they decide to question this assumption and remain open to other possibilities.

Starting from Zero: Instead of continuing with their existing workout regimen, the individual decides to start from scratch. They take some time to research different approaches to fitness and health.

Innovative Goal Setting: During their research, the individual discovers new fitness trends and strategies. They decide to set a goal of improving their physical fitness by exploring a variety of exercise routines, including yoga, high-intensity interval training (HIIT), and outdoor activities like hiking.

Efficiency and Effectiveness: As they explore different fitness activities, the individual identifies which ones align best with their fitness goals and schedule. They find that HIIT workouts provide efficient results within their time constraints.

Continuous Improvement: The individual regularly assesses their progress and makes adjustments to their fitness routine. If they plateau or lose motivation, they explore other activities or consult with a fitness expert for guidance.

By incorporating ZBT principles into their goal-setting process:

The individual avoids complacency and is open to trying new approaches.

Decision-making is driven by the pursuit of more efficient and effective strategies.

The individual maintains a commitment to continuous improvement in achieving their fitness goals.

This example demonstrates how ZBT can be applied to personal goal setting, resulting in a more innovative, efficient, and adaptable approach to achieving objectives. Whether it's fitness, career goals, or personal development, ZBT can help individuals break free from assumptions and find creative pathways to success.

Time Management

Time management is an area where Zero-Based Thinking (ZBT) can significantly impact an individual's productivity and effectiveness. ZBT encourages individuals to reevaluate their daily routines and schedules, prioritize tasks, and allocate time based on current goals and objectives. This approach can lead to a more efficient and productive use of time. Here's an expansion of this concept, along with an illustrative example:

Routine Reevaluation: ZBT begins with a critical assessment of an individual's daily routines and time allocation. This includes questioning the necessity and value of recurring tasks and habits.

Starting from Zero: Instead of assuming that existing time management practices are optimal, individuals start with a blank slate. They consider how they can design their daily schedules to better align with their current goals and priorities.

Task Prioritization: ZBT prompts individuals to prioritize tasks and activities based on their importance and relevance to their goals. This ensures that valuable time is allocated to high-impact activities.

Efficient Time Allocation: By reevaluating their time management, individuals can identify opportunities to allocate time more efficiently. This may involve time blocking, delegation, or eliminating time-wasting activities.

Goal Alignment: ZBT emphasizes aligning daily routines with overarching goals and objectives. It encourages individuals to focus on tasks that contribute directly to their desired outcomes.

Example

Let's consider how a professional applies ZBT to improve their time management:

Challenge: The professional feels overwhelmed by their workload and struggles to balance their professional and personal life effectively.

Routine Reevaluation: The professional realizes that their current routine includes many non-essential tasks that consume valuable time. They decide to critically assess their daily habits.

Starting from Zero: Instead of continuing with their existing schedule, they decide to create a new daily routine from scratch, considering their current work responsibilities, personal goals, and well-being.

Task Prioritization: Through ZBT, they identify the most critical tasks that directly contribute to their career growth and personal development. They prioritize these tasks over less important ones.

Efficient Time Allocation: The professional finds that they spend a significant amount of time on emails and meetings. They decide to implement time blocking for focused work and reduce the frequency and duration of non-essential meetings.

Goal Alignment: They ensure that their daily routine aligns with their long-term goals, such as improving job performance, pursuing further education, and maintaining a healthy work-life balance.

By incorporating ZBT principles into their time management:

The professional avoids getting stuck in unproductive routines and is open to more effective time allocation strategies.

Decision-making is guided by the goal of optimizing productivity and achieving both professional and personal objectives.

The professional achieves a more balanced and fulfilling daily routine that contributes to their overall success and well-being.

This example illustrates how ZBT can be applied to time management, resulting in a more purposeful, goal-oriented, and efficient use of time. Whether it's in a professional context or personal life, ZBT helps individuals make informed decisions about how they allocate their time to achieve their desired outcomes.

Problem-Solving

Problem-solving is an area where Zero-Based Thinking (ZBT) can be a valuable approach. ZBT encourages individuals to approach problems with a fresh perspective, challenging assumptions and exploring unconventional solutions. This approach can lead to more innovative and effective problem-solving. Here's an expansion of this concept, along with an illustrative example:

Breaking Free from Habitual Thinking: ZBT begins by encouraging individuals to break free from habitual thinking patterns. Instead of relying on familiar solutions, they question whether there are better alternatives.

Questioning Assumptions: ZBT prompts individuals to question the assumptions they make when approaching a problem. This includes assumptions about the nature of the problem, the causes, and the potential solutions.

Starting from Zero: Rather than assuming that past solutions will work, individuals start with a clean slate. They consider the problem as if they've never encountered it before and explore new angles.

Exploration of Unconventional Solutions: ZBT encourages individuals to think beyond the conventional boundaries. They explore creative and unconventional solutions that might not have been considered if they were confined by their existing mental frameworks.

Efficiency and Innovation: By challenging established practices, ZBT can lead to more efficient and innovative problem-solving. It allows individuals to identify and eliminate inefficiencies and allocate resources more effectively.

Example

Let's consider how an individual applies ZBT to solve a personal challenge:

Challenge: The individual has been struggling with time management and feels overwhelmed by their daily tasks and responsibilities.

Breaking Free from Habitual Thinking: The individual realizes that they've been using the same time management techniques for years without significant improvement. They decide it's time for a change.

Questioning Assumptions: They question the assumption that their current workload and responsibilities must be managed in the same way. They also question whether multitasking is truly effective.

Starting from Zero: Instead of relying on their existing time management methods, they decide to approach the problem as if they've never tried to manage their time before.

Exploration of Unconventional Solutions: They explore unconventional solutions like time-blocking, which involves allocating specific blocks of time to different tasks and focusing on one task at a time. This is a departure from their habit of juggling multiple tasks simultaneously.

Efficiency and Innovation: By adopting the time-blocking method and giving it a fair chance, they find that they are more focused and efficient. They eliminate the inefficiency of context switching and improve their productivity.

By incorporating ZBT principles into their problem-solving approach:

The individual breaks free from their old, ineffective time management habits.

Decision-making is guided by a commitment to find more efficient and innovative solutions.

The individual achieves better time management and reduced feelings of overwhelm.

This example demonstrates how ZBT can be applied to personal problem-solving, leading to more effective and innovative solutions. Whether it's addressing time management issues, overcoming personal challenges, or making important life decisions, ZBT encourages individuals to approach problems with fresh eyes and an open mind, ultimately fostering more efficient and creative solutions.

Lifestyle Choices

Lifestyle choices, including diet, exercise, and personal habits, play a crucial role in an individual's overall well-being and health. Zero-Based Thinking (ZBT) can be a transformative approach when applied to lifestyle choices, encouraging individuals to reevaluate and improve their habits for a healthier and more fulfilling life. Here's an expansion of this concept, along with an illustrative example:

Breaking Free from Habitual Choices: ZBT begins by prompting individuals to break free from ingrained or habitual lifestyle choices that may not be serving their best interests.

Questioning Assumptions: Individuals are encouraged to question assumptions they have about their current lifestyle choices. This includes examining beliefs about what constitutes a healthy diet, effective exercise, or positive personal habits.

Starting from Zero: Instead of relying on past choices, individuals start with a clean slate. They approach their lifestyle as if they have no preconceived notions and are open to exploring new options.

Exploration of Healthier Choices: ZBT encourages individuals to explore healthier, more sustainable, or more fulfilling lifestyle choices. This may involve trying new diets, exercise routines, or personal development practices.

Efficiency and Well-Being: By reevaluating and improving their lifestyle choices, individuals can experience improved physical and mental well-being. They may also discover more efficient ways to maintain a healthy lifestyle.

Example: Let's consider how an individual applies ZBT to their diet and exercise choices:

Challenge: The individual has struggled with maintaining a healthy diet and exercise routine due to busy work schedules and occasional emotional eating.

Breaking Free from Habitual Choices: The individual acknowledges that their habitual diet choices often involve fast food and stress-induced snacking, which is negatively affecting their health and energy levels.

Questioning Assumptions: They question the assumption that convenience foods are the only option during busy workdays and that emotional eating is an effective coping mechanism for stress.

Starting from Zero: They decide to approach their diet and exercise choices as if they've never considered them before.

Exploration of Healthier Choices: They explore healthier dietary options that can be prepared quickly, such as meal prepping and choosing nutrient-dense snacks. They also investigate stress-management techniques like meditation and regular exercise.

Efficiency and Well-Being: By adopting these new choices, the individual experiences increased energy, improved mood, and better physical health. They find that healthier eating habits and stress-management practices are more efficient in maintaining their well-being.

By incorporating ZBT principles into their lifestyle choices:

The individual breaks free from unhealthy dietary and coping habits.

Decision-making is guided by a commitment to exploring healthier and more efficient lifestyle choices.

[181]

The individual achieves improved physical and mental well-being through their new lifestyle choices.

This example illustrates how ZBT can be applied to lifestyle choices, leading to healthier and more sustainable habits. Whether it's dietary choices, exercise routines, or personal habits, ZBT encourages individuals to reevaluate and improve their lifestyles for greater overall well-being and satisfaction.

Career Planning

Career planning is a critical aspect of personal and professional development. Zero-Based Thinking (ZBT) can be a powerful approach when applied to career planning, encouraging individuals to reassess their career goals, skills, and development plans to ensure alignment with current aspirations and market demands. Here's an expansion of this concept, along with an illustrative example:

Breaking Free from Inertia: ZBT begins by prompting individuals to break free from inertia or complacency in their current career path. This may involve challenging the assumption that their current job or career trajectory is the only viable option.

Questioning Assumptions: Individuals are encouraged to question assumptions they have about their career goals, skills, and development plans. This includes examining beliefs about the path they "should" follow.

Starting from Zero: Instead of assuming that their current career path is optimal, individuals start with a clean slate. They approach career planning as if they are just beginning their professional journey and consider new possibilities.

Exploration of Aspirations: ZBT encourages individuals to explore their current career aspirations and evaluate whether these aspirations align with their values, interests, and market demands. This may involve setting new career goals or refining existing ones.

Efficiency and Adaptability: By reevaluating and adapting their career plans, individuals can ensure that they are on a path that is both personally fulfilling and aligned with current market demands. This may involve acquiring new skills or adjusting their professional trajectory.

Example

Let's consider how an individual applies ZBT to their career planning:

Challenge: The individual has been working in a specific industry for several years but is beginning to feel unfulfilled and uncertain about their long-term career goals.

Breaking Free from Inertia: The individual recognizes that they have been staying in their current job out of habit and a fear of change. They acknowledge their dissatisfaction and the need for a change.

Questioning Assumptions: They question the assumption that they must stay in their current industry due to their past experience. They also question the belief that job security is more important than career fulfillment.

Starting from Zero: They decide to approach their career planning as if they are just beginning their professional journey and are open to exploring different career options.

Exploration of Aspirations: Through self-reflection and research, they discover a new interest in a different field that aligns better with their values and interests. They set new career goals related to entering this field.

Efficiency and Adaptability: The individual invests in further education and skill development to make the transition into their desired field more efficient and successful.

By incorporating ZBT principles into their career planning:

The individual breaks free from career inertia and is open to exploring new possibilities.

Decision-making is guided by a commitment to aligning career aspirations with personal fulfillment and market demands.

[184]

The individual achieves a more fulfilling and adaptable career path that aligns with their current goals and interests.

This example demonstrates how ZBT can be applied to career planning, leading to more fulfilling and adaptable career trajectories. Whether it's exploring new industries, acquiring new skills, or pursuing different career goals, ZBT encourages individuals to make informed decisions that align with their evolving aspirations and market conditions.

Best Practices

Zero-Based Thinking (ZBT) is a valuable approach in many scenarios, but it's essential to recognize that it may not be the best fit for every situation. The choice to use ZBT should be based on a thoughtful consideration of the specific context and objectives of the decision-making process.

When Zero Based Thinking Isn't the Right Choice

Zero-Based Thinking is a valuable approach for challenging the status quo, fostering innovation, and ensuring that decisions align with current goals and objectives. However, its suitability varies depending on the specific circumstances. Deciding whether to use ZBT or not should be a thoughtful and context-driven choice, taking into account the nature of the problem, available resources, time constraints, and the desired outcomes of the decision-making process.

Well-Established Best Practices: ZBT may not be necessary when well-established best practices exist for a particular process or problem. In such cases, building upon existing knowledge and practices can be efficient and effective, as these practices have been refined over time to yield optimal results.

Limited Resources or Time Constraints: ZBT can be resource-intensive and time-consuming. If an organization or individual faces tight deadlines or has limited resources, starting from scratch and thoroughly evaluating every aspect of a situation may not be practical. In these cases, it may be more efficient to rely on existing knowledge and practices.

Low-Impact Decisions: Not every decision or problem requires the level of scrutiny and analysis that ZBT demands. For low-impact decisions or routine tasks, the benefits gained from starting from zero may not outweigh the associated costs and efforts. In these situations, it's often more practical to rely on established routines and processes.

Historical Data Availability: ZBT may not be suitable when historical data is readily available and relevant. If past performance data or benchmarking information can provide valuable insights into decision-making, it might be more efficient to use this data as a starting point rather than beginning from scratch.

Complexity vs. Simplicity: The complexity of the problem or decision at hand is an important factor to consider. ZBT is particularly useful for complex problems that benefit from a fresh perspective and innovative solutions. However, for straightforward and uncomplicated matters, a more straightforward decision-making process may suffice.

Cultural and Organizational Factors: ZBT may face resistance in organizational cultures that are highly risk-averse or strongly tied to tradition. If an organization values stability and continuity over innovation, ZBT might not align with its cultural norms.

Value of Incremental Improvements: In situations where incremental improvements are sufficient to meet objectives, there may be little need for the radical changes that ZBT can bring. Incremental improvements can be achieved by building upon existing practices without starting from zero.

Resource Efficiency: Organizations and individuals must consider the trade-offs between the resources (time, money, personnel) required to implement ZBT versus the potential benefits it offers. In some cases, it may be more resource-efficient to optimize existing processes rather than reinventing them.

Zero-Based Thinking Applications

Here are ten real-world examples of Zero-Based Thinking (ZBT) applied in various contexts. These examples illustrate the versatility of ZBT as a problem-solving and decision-making approach applicable in various domains, including finance, operations, marketing, education, and healthcare, among others. It encourages a critical examination of existing practices and the pursuit of more efficient and effective solutions.

Cost Management in a Corporation

Expanding on the application of Zero-Based Thinking (ZBT) in cost management within a large corporation:

Detailed Expense Evaluation: In a typical budgeting process, organizations often start with the previous year's budget as a baseline and make adjustments as needed. However, in the case of ZBT, each department is tasked with evaluating every line item and expense thoroughly. This means going through expenses one by one, questioning their necessity, and providing a valid reason for each cost.

Identification of Redundancies: One of the key benefits of ZBT in cost management is its ability to uncover redundant expenses. By requiring departments to justify every cost, the corporation can identify instances where multiple departments may be duplicating efforts or where different departments are purchasing similar services or resources independently.

Alignment with Strategic Goals: ZBT ensures that expenses are closely aligned with the company's strategic goals and objectives. Each department must demonstrate how its expenses contribute to the overall success of the organization. This alignment helps prioritize expenditures that directly impact the company's mission and profitability.

Resource Reallocation: As departments justify their expenses, ZBT allows for resource reallocation based on strategic priorities. If certain expenses are deemed less critical, the funds can be shifted to initiatives that offer a higher return on investment or are more aligned with the company's long-term strategy.

Enhanced Efficiency: Through ZBT, the corporation encourages a culture of efficiency and cost-consciousness. Departments become more aware of the financial implications of their decisions, leading to more prudent resource utilization. This focus on efficiency can result in cost savings and improved profitability.

Reduction of Waste: ZBT is effective in identifying and reducing waste within the organization. Unnecessary or non-value-added expenses are more likely to be exposed and eliminated when each expenditure is scrutinized. This waste reduction contributes to a leaner and more competitive organization.

Risk Mitigation: ZBT's careful evaluation of expenses also considers potential risks associated with each cost. This risk assessment allows the corporation to proactively address vulnerabilities and develop contingency plans, ensuring that potential financial risks are managed effectively.

Continuous Improvement: ZBT is not a one-time exercise but an ongoing process. It promotes a culture of continuous improvement, where budgeting and expense evaluation are regularly revisited to adapt to changing market conditions, business strategies, and financial goals.

Communication and Accountability: ZBT fosters transparency and accountability within the organization. Each department is responsible for justifying its expenses, and this information is communicated across the organization. This transparency helps build trust and ensures that resources are allocated responsibly.

Competitive Advantage: By implementing ZBT in cost management, the corporation can gain a competitive advantage. It becomes more agile and better equipped to adapt to market shifts and economic fluctuations, ensuring its long-term sustainability and profitability.

Zero-Based Thinking applied to cost management in a corporation is a strategic approach that goes beyond traditional budgeting. It encourages a meticulous review of expenses, fosters efficiency, promotes strategic alignment, and drives a culture of continuous improvement—all of which contribute to the organization's financial health and competitive position in the market.

Personal Finance

Expanding on the application of Zero-Based Thinking (ZBT) to personal finance:

Starting from Scratch: In personal finance, ZBT involves approaching one's financial situation with a clean slate. Instead of relying on existing spending patterns and habits, the individual starts with a blank budget sheet. This signifies a commitment to reevaluate every financial decision and expenditure from the ground up.

Holistic Expense Analysis: The heart of ZBT in personal finance is a comprehensive and detailed analysis of every expense. This entails going through each item in the budget, no matter how small, and questioning its necessity and alignment with the individual's current financial objectives. It's an opportunity to scrutinize spending habits and identify areas for improvement.

Alignment with Financial Goals: ZBT emphasizes that every expense should contribute to achieving specific financial goals. Whether it's saving for retirement, paying off debt, building an emergency fund, or pursuing a major purchase, each expense must be evaluated based on its ability to support these objectives. This alignment ensures that resources are directed toward what matters most to the individual.

Prioritizing Needs vs. Wants: ZBT encourages individuals to differentiate between needs and wants. It prompts a thorough examination of expenses to determine whether they are essential for daily living or discretionary luxuries. This helps individuals make conscious choices about where to allocate their financial resources.

Expense Reduction: By scrutinizing each expense, ZBT often leads to the identification of unnecessary or excessive costs. This process can result in expense reduction through cutting out non-essential items, negotiating better rates, or finding more cost-effective alternatives.

Budget Flexibility: While ZBT encourages a thorough evaluation of expenses, it also recognizes the importance of flexibility. Individuals may find that some expenses are non-negotiable, such as housing, utilities, and essential groceries. ZBT allows for these necessary expenses while encouraging optimization elsewhere.

Risk Assessment and Contingency Planning: ZBT in personal finance extends to assessing financial risks and planning for contingencies. Individuals consider potential financial risks such as job loss, unexpected medical expenses, or changes in income. They then develop contingency plans, like building an emergency fund, to mitigate these risks.

Savings and Investment Review: Beyond daily expenses, ZBT encourages individuals to review their savings and investment strategies. They assess whether their current approach aligns with their long-term financial goals, such as retirement planning and wealth accumulation. Adjustments may be made to optimize these aspects of personal finance.

Financial Literacy and Education: Implementing ZBT in personal finance often requires individuals to improve their financial literacy. They may need to educate themselves about budgeting, investing, debt management, and other financial topics to make informed decisions.

Regular Reevaluation: ZBT is not a one-time exercise; it's a continuous process. Individuals should periodically revisit and update their budget, taking into account changes in income, expenses, and financial goals. This ensures that their financial plan remains aligned with their evolving needs and objectives.

Zero-Based Thinking applied to personal finance is a proactive approach that empowers individuals to take control of their financial well-being. It promotes a systematic review of expenses, a focus on financial goals, and a commitment to making conscious and informed financial decisions, ultimately leading to a more secure and financially fulfilling life.

Supply Chain Optimization

Expanding on the application of Zero-Based Thinking (ZBT) to supply chain optimization within a manufacturing company:

Comprehensive Supplier Assessment: In the context of supply chain management, ZBT prompts the manufacturing company to evaluate every aspect of its supplier relationships. This includes assessing the reliability, quality, cost-effectiveness, and responsiveness of each supplier. By scrutinizing each supplier, the company ensures that it is working with partners who align with its strategic objectives.

Logistics Cost Analysis: ZBT requires a thorough examination of logistics costs, including transportation, warehousing, and distribution expenses. The company reviews transportation modes, routes, and carrier contracts to identify potential cost-saving opportunities. This analysis may lead to optimizing shipping methods, renegotiating contracts, or considering alternative logistics providers.

Inventory Management: ZBT also extends to the company's inventory management practices. The organization evaluates its inventory levels, turnover rates, and holding costs for each product or component. This analysis helps identify slow-moving items, excess inventory, or opportunities to implement just-in-time inventory practices, reducing carrying costs and freeing up working capital.

Sourcing Strategies: By starting from scratch with ZBT, the company assesses its sourcing strategies for raw materials and components. This may involve exploring alternative suppliers, considering local sourcing options, or reevaluating global supply chains for resilience and cost-effectiveness.

Demand Forecasting: ZBT encourages a fresh look at demand forecasting methodologies. The company assesses its forecasting accuracy, the tools and technologies used, and the alignment of forecasts with actual market demand. Improving demand forecasting accuracy can lead to more efficient production planning and inventory management.

Risk Mitigation: Supply chain risks, such as disruptions due to natural disasters, geopolitical events, or economic fluctuations, are a significant consideration. ZBT incorporates risk assessment into supply chain optimization by identifying vulnerabilities and developing contingency plans to mitigate potential disruptions.

Technology Integration: Modern supply chain optimization often involves leveraging advanced technologies such as data analytics, Internet of Things (IoT) sensors, and artificial intelligence. ZBT encourages the exploration of cutting-edge technologies that can enhance supply chain visibility, efficiency, and responsiveness.

Sustainability and Environmental Impact: ZBT may prompt the company to evaluate the environmental impact of its supply chain practices. This includes assessing carbon emissions, waste generation, and resource utilization. The company can then explore eco-friendly alternatives, such as sustainable sourcing and green logistics options.

Continuous Improvement Culture: Implementing ZBT in supply chain management fosters a culture of continuous improvement. Teams are encouraged to regularly reassess supply chain practices and adapt to changing market conditions, customer demands, and technological advancements.

Supplier Diversity and Ethical Practices: ZBT encourages companies to examine supplier diversity and ethical practices. Organizations assess whether their supplier base represents diverse perspectives and values. This evaluation can lead to efforts to enhance supplier diversity and ensure that suppliers adhere to ethical and responsible business practices.

Zero-Based Thinking applied to supply chain optimization is a strategic approach that enables manufacturing companies to reevaluate every aspect of their supply chain. It promotes efficiency, cost-effectiveness, resilience, and alignment with strategic objectives, ultimately leading to a more competitive and agile supply chain that can better respond to market dynamics and customer demands.

Nonprofit Organization

The application of Zero-Based Thinking (ZBT) to program optimization within a nonprofit organization:

Mission Alignment: The foundation of ZBT in a nonprofit context is a commitment to mission alignment. Instead of taking existing programs for granted, the organization begins with a clear understanding of its mission and goals. It then evaluates each program to determine how effectively it contributes to the mission.

Comprehensive Program Assessment: ZBT necessitates a comprehensive assessment of all existing programs. This includes evaluating program objectives, outcomes, costs, and resource utilization. Programs are analyzed in terms of their relevance to the organization's mission, their impact on the target audience, and their cost-effectiveness.

Outcome Measurement: A critical component of ZBT in nonprofits is measuring outcomes and impact. The organization sets specific metrics and key performance indicators (KPIs) for each program, ensuring that there is a quantifiable way to assess its success. Programs that do not meet these criteria are subject to reevaluation.

Resource Allocation: ZBT encourages the nonprofit to reallocate resources based on the assessment of each program's impact. If certain programs are found to have a more significant and measurable positive effect on the mission, resources can be redirected from less effective programs to those with a higher return on investment.

Program Redundancies: During the ZBT process, the nonprofit identifies any redundancies or overlapping efforts among its programs. This allows for streamlining and consolidation, reducing administrative overhead and ensuring that resources are concentrated where they have the most impact.

Innovation and New Initiatives: ZBT may lead to the development of new initiatives or the expansion of programs that have proven to be particularly effective. By freeing up resources from underperforming programs, the organization has the flexibility to invest in innovative solutions and reach new target audiences.

Stakeholder Involvement: ZBT often involves input from various stakeholders, including program beneficiaries, donors, staff, and board members. Engaging these stakeholders in the decision-making process ensures that program optimization aligns with the needs and expectations of the organization's supporters and those it serves.

Strategic Planning Integration: The findings of ZBT can inform the organization's strategic planning process. By optimizing programs to align with the mission and strategic goals, the nonprofit ensures that its resources and efforts are focused on achieving long-term impact.

Transparency and Accountability: ZBT promotes transparency and accountability within the nonprofit. As the organization publicly reevaluates and reallocates resources among programs, it builds trust with donors and supporters, demonstrating responsible stewardship of funds.

Continuous Monitoring and Evaluation: ZBT is not a one-time exercise; it's an ongoing process. Nonprofits regularly monitor and evaluate their programs, adjusting them as needed to adapt to changing circumstances, emerging needs, and evolving best practices.

Zero-Based Thinking applied to program optimization in nonprofit organizations is a strategic approach that ensures resources are directed toward initiatives that align most closely with the organization's mission and deliver measurable impact. It encourages continuous improvement, innovation, and transparency, ultimately leading to a more effective and efficient use of resources in pursuit of the organization's charitable goals.

Healthcare Services

Expanding on the application of Zero-Based Thinking (ZBT) in healthcare services within a hospital:

Clinical Department Assessment: ZBT prompts the hospital to review every clinical department, evaluating the necessity and effectiveness of each. This includes medical, surgical, and diagnostic departments, as well as specialized units like intensive care and radiology. The goal is to ensure that each department aligns with the hospital's mission of providing high-quality care.

Equipment Evaluation: ZBT extends to a thorough evaluation of the hospital's medical equipment. This includes medical devices, diagnostic tools, and imaging equipment. Each piece of equipment is assessed for its clinical utility, maintenance costs, and its contribution to patient outcomes. Outdated or underutilized equipment may be identified for replacement or consolidation.

Procedures and Protocols: ZBT encourages a critical examination of medical procedures and clinical protocols. Hospital administrators and healthcare providers review existing practices, considering factors such as clinical evidence, patient outcomes, and cost-effectiveness. This process may lead to the refinement of protocols or the adoption of new best practices.

Resource Allocation: The hospital reallocates resources based on the ZBT assessment. If certain clinical departments or services are found to be less essential or less effective, resources can be shifted to departments or services that have a more significant positive impact on patient care and outcomes. This ensures efficient resource allocation.

Patient-Centered Care: ZBT emphasizes the importance of patient-centered care. Hospital administrators consider how each decision impacts patient well-being, experience, and safety. The assessment process aims to enhance the overall quality of care provided while reducing any unnecessary costs or inefficiencies that may affect patients.

Care Continuum and Integration: Hospitals often evaluate how different departments and services work together to provide a seamless care continuum. ZBT encourages the optimization of care pathways to improve patient outcomes and experiences. This might involve integrating services, reducing duplications, and enhancing care coordination.

Staffing and Training: ZBT in healthcare services also involves assessing staffing levels and training requirements. The hospital evaluates the skillsets and qualifications of its healthcare staff to ensure that the workforce aligns with the hospital's evolving needs and strategic goals. Adjustments may be made in staffing and training programs to enhance efficiency and quality.

Technology and Information Systems: Modern 4healthcare relies heavily on technology and information systems. ZBT promotes an assessment of these systems to determine their effectiveness, security, and contribution to patient care. Hospitals may invest in new technology or optimize existing systems to improve patient care and reduce operational costs.

Regulatory Compliance: Compliance with healthcare regulations and standards is paramount. ZBT ensures that the hospital continues to meet or exceed regulatory requirements while seeking opportunities to streamline compliance efforts and reduce associated costs.

Continuous Improvement Culture: ZBT fosters a culture of continuous improvement within the hospital. Healthcare providers and administrators are encouraged to regularly reassess healthcare services, adapt to emerging medical practices, and respond to changing patient needs, ensuring that the hospital remains at the forefront of healthcare excellence.

Zero-Based Thinking applied to healthcare services in a hospital aims to provide the best quality care to patients while optimizing resource allocation and reducing unnecessary costs. It promotes a patient-centered approach, evidence-based decision-making, and a commitment to continuous improvement in healthcare delivery.

Marketing Campaign

Expanding on the application of Zero-Based Thinking (ZBT) in marketing campaign development:

Fresh Audience Analysis: In a ZBT-driven marketing campaign, the marketing team begins with a fresh audience analysis. This involves reevaluating the target audience demographics, behaviors, preferences, and pain points. The team refrains from making assumptions based on previous campaigns and ensures that they have an up-to-date understanding of their audience.

Market Research: ZBT encourages comprehensive market research to identify emerging trends, consumer sentiments, and competitive landscape. The marketing team conducts new market research to gather data that may lead to innovative insights and a deeper understanding of customer needs.

Messaging Reimagination: Rather than relying on preexisting messaging templates, ZBT prompts the marketing team to reimagine the campaign message. They consider how to convey the brand's value proposition, mission, and unique selling points in a fresh and compelling way. This creative approach aims to capture the audience's attention and resonate with their emotions.

Content Creation: ZBT encourages the development of new and engaging content. The team explores innovative content formats, storytelling techniques, and visuals to convey the campaign message effectively. This can include video content, interactive experiences, user-generated content campaigns, and more.

Channel Selection: In the context of ZBT, the marketing team critically evaluates the choice of advertising channels. Instead of defaulting to the same channels used in past campaigns, they explore new and emerging platforms that may offer a better fit for reaching the target audience. This can include social media, influencer marketing, content partnerships, and niche advertising networks.

Budget Justification: ZBT requires the marketing team to justify the budget allocation for each element of the campaign. This ensures that every expense, whether it's related to advertising, creative production, or technology tools, is directly tied to achieving campaign objectives and maximizing return on investment (ROI).

Measurement Metrics: The team establishes clear and relevant key performance indicators (KPIs) specific to the campaign's objectives. ZBT emphasizes that these metrics should be tied to the campaign's innovative aspects and goals, whether it's audience engagement, conversion rates, brand awareness, or other desired outcomes.

A/B Testing and Experimentation: ZBT promotes a culture of experimentation and A/B testing. The marketing team designs controlled experiments to assess the effectiveness of different campaign elements, such as messaging variants, creative assets, or channel combinations. This data-driven approach allows for continuous improvement throughout the campaign.

Feedback Loops: ZBT encourages the marketing team to establish feedback loops with the target audience. This can involve surveys, focus groups, or social media monitoring to gather real-time insights and adjust the campaign strategy as needed to better resonate with the audience.

Adaptability and Flexibility: ZBT recognizes that market conditions can change rapidly. The marketing team remains adaptable and flexible, ready to adjust the campaign strategy in response to emerging trends, competitor actions, or unforeseen circumstances.

Zero-Based Thinking applied to marketing campaign development promotes a forward-thinking and innovative approach. It encourages marketing teams to question established practices, leverage new data and insights, and continuously experiment to create campaigns that are not only effective but also fresh, engaging, and memorable in the eyes of their target audience.

Energy Efficiency in a Building

The application of Zero-Based Thinking (ZBT) in improving energy efficiency in a commercial building managed by a property management company:

Comprehensive Energy Audit: ZBT prompts the property management company to conduct a comprehensive energy audit of the building. This involves a detailed assessment of energy consumption across all systems and areas of the property, including lighting, heating, ventilation, and air conditioning (HVAC), appliances, and insulation.

Data Analysis: The property management team analyzes historical energy consumption data to identify trends and patterns. They also compare the building's energy performance to industry benchmarks and best practices to gain insights into potential areas for improvement.

Energy Consumption Assessment: ZBT requires a critical examination of energy-consuming equipment and systems. The property management team evaluates the efficiency of lighting fixtures, HVAC units, water heaters, and other appliances. This assessment helps pinpoint which systems are outdated, inefficient, or in need of maintenance or replacement.

Lighting Efficiency: ZBT places a specific focus on lighting. The property management company explores opportunities to upgrade to energy-efficient lighting technologies, such as LED bulbs and smart lighting controls. They also consider daylight harvesting and occupancy sensors to reduce unnecessary lighting usage.

HVAC Optimization: HVAC systems often account for a significant portion of a building's energy consumption. ZBT encourages the evaluation of HVAC efficiency through measures such as system zoning, regular maintenance, upgrading to energy-efficient models, and the use of programmable thermostats to better control heating and cooling.

Insulation and Building Envelope: The property management team assesses the building's insulation and overall envelope integrity. Proper insulation and sealing gaps or leaks can significantly reduce heating and cooling demands, leading to substantial energy savings.

Renewable Energy Integration: ZBT encourages exploring the integration of renewable energy sources, such as solar panels or wind turbines, into the building's energy mix. This allows the property to generate clean energy on-site, reducing reliance on grid-supplied electricity.

Behavioral Changes: ZBT emphasizes the role of occupants in energy efficiency. The property management company may implement educational programs and incentives to encourage energy-conscious behavior among building occupants, such as turning off lights when not in use or using energy-efficient appliances.

Energy-Efficient Building Design: If applicable, ZBT may lead to a reevaluation of the building's design. When planning renovations or new construction, the property management company can prioritize energy-efficient architectural features and materials.

Cost-Benefit Analysis: ZBT involves conducting cost-benefit analyses for potential energy efficiency improvements. The property management team evaluates the upfront costs of upgrades against the expected energy savings and return on investment over time. This ensures that investments align with long-term financial goals.

Sustainability Certification: ZBT may lead to pursuing sustainability certifications, such as LEED (Leadership in Energy and Environmental Design) or ENERGY STAR. These certifications can validate the building's energy efficiency efforts and enhance its marketability.

Continuous Monitoring and Optimization: ZBT is an ongoing process. The property management company establishes a system for continuous monitoring of energy consumption, allowing them to identify deviations from expected performance and implement timely adjustments to maintain and improve energy efficiency.

Zero-Based Thinking applied to energy efficiency in a commercial building promotes a comprehensive and proactive approach to reduce energy consumption, lower operational costs, and contribute to environmental sustainability. It encourages the property management company to challenge established energy practices and explore innovative solutions to optimize building performance.

Educational Curriculum Development

Expanding on the application of Zero-Based Thinking (ZBT) in educational curriculum development within a school district:

Curriculum Redesign Philosophy: ZBT in curriculum development signifies a fundamental shift in the approach to education. Instead of simply building upon existing curriculum structures, educators and administrators begin with the premise that the entire curriculum needs to be reevaluated and redesigned to meet current educational standards and objectives.

Alignment with Modern Standards: ZBT places a strong emphasis on ensuring that the curriculum aligns with the latest educational standards and requirements. This involves a careful examination of state, national, and global standards to ensure that what students learn is relevant and prepares them for the challenges of the modern world.

Identifying Essential Learning Outcomes: Educators and curriculum developers use ZBT to identify the core learning outcomes that are essential for students to master. This involves a systematic review of educational goals, cognitive skills, and competencies that students need to succeed academically and in their future careers.

Subject and Topic Reevaluation: ZBT encourages a fresh look at the subjects and topics covered in the curriculum. Educators assess the relevance and importance of each subject, considering the changing needs of students and society. Outdated or less relevant topics may be replaced with new subjects that reflect emerging knowledge and skills.

Interdisciplinary Integration: ZBT promotes the integration of subjects and topics across disciplines. Educators explore ways to create a more holistic and interconnected curriculum that emphasizes critical thinking, problem-solving, and the application of knowledge in real-world scenarios.

Teaching Methods and Pedagogy: In the spirit of ZBT, educators reconsider their teaching methods and pedagogical approaches. They explore innovative teaching techniques, technology integration, and experiential learning opportunities that engage students and enhance their understanding of the curriculum.

Learning Resources: ZBT prompts a review of learning resources and materials. Educators assess textbooks, digital resources, and educational tools to ensure they align with the redefined curriculum objectives. Outdated or ineffective resources may be replaced with more relevant and engaging materials.

Assessment Strategies: The school district reevaluates its assessment strategies to align with the redesigned curriculum. This includes developing new assessment methods that accurately measure students' mastery of essential learning outcomes and encourage critical thinking and problem-solving skills.

Professional Development: ZBT recognizes the importance of equipping educators with the knowledge and skills needed to implement the redesigned curriculum effectively. The school district invests in professional development programs that empower teachers to deliver the curriculum in innovative and engaging ways.

Stakeholder Involvement: ZBT encourages the involvement of various stakeholders, including teachers, parents, students, and community members, in the curriculum development process. This ensures that the curriculum reflects the diverse needs and perspectives of the educational community.

Pilot Programs and Iterative Development: The school district may implement pilot programs to test the effectiveness of the redesigned curriculum. Feedback from teachers, students, and parents is used to make iterative improvements, ensuring that the curriculum evolves and remains responsive to changing educational needs.

Lifelong Learning Emphasis: ZBT encourages the inclusion of lifelong learning skills and competencies in the curriculum. Educators aim to prepare students not only for academic success but also for a lifetime of learning, adaptability, and skill development.

Zero-Based Thinking applied to educational curriculum development represents a forward-thinking and flexible approach. It prioritizes relevance, adaptability, and alignment with modern educational standards and aims to equip students with the knowledge, skills, and attitudes needed to thrive in an ever-changing world.

Agricultural Practices

The application of Zero-Based Thinking (ZBT) in optimizing crop cultivation within agriculture:

Holistic Soil Analysis: ZBT prompts the farmer to begin with a comprehensive analysis of soil conditions. This involves assessing soil health, composition, nutrient levels, pH balance, and organic matter content. The goal is to gain a deep understanding of the soil's current state as the foundation for informed decisions.

Crop Selection Reevaluation: Rather than defaulting to traditional crop choices, the farmer critically evaluates crop selection. ZBT encourages exploring a diverse range of crops and considering factors such as market demand, climate suitability, and crop rotation benefits. The aim is to select crops that maximize yield, market value, and resource conservation.

Irrigation Efficiency: ZBT emphasizes efficient water management. The farmer assesses irrigation techniques, exploring options such as drip irrigation, precision irrigation, or rainwater harvesting systems. This evaluation aims to reduce water wastage, optimize irrigation schedules, and improve water use efficiency.

Soil Improvement Strategies: ZBT encourages a proactive approach to soil improvement. The farmer explores soil enrichment methods, such as cover cropping, crop residue management, and organic matter addition. These practices enhance soil fertility, structure, and moisture retention, ultimately leading to improved crop yields.

Integrated Pest Management (IPM): The farmer adopts an IPM approach, which involves reevaluating pest and disease control methods. ZBT promotes the use of environmentally friendly and sustainable pest management strategies, minimizing the need for chemical pesticides and reducing environmental impacts.

Crop Rotation and Diversity: ZBT highlights the benefits of crop rotation and diversification. The farmer plans crop rotations strategically to break pest cycles, enhance soil health, and optimize nutrient utilization. This approach also helps reduce the risk of crop failure due to pests or adverse weather conditions.

Resource Allocation: The farmer allocates resources wisely based on the ZBT assessment. This includes optimizing the use of fertilizers, pesticides, and other inputs to match the specific needs of crops and soil conditions. Resource allocation is guided by cost-effectiveness and environmental sustainability.

Technology Integration: ZBT encourages the integration of modern agricultural technologies. The farmer explores the use of data-driven solutions, such as precision agriculture and sensor-based monitoring, to make informed decisions about planting, harvesting, and resource management.

Environmental Stewardship: ZBT promotes responsible environmental practices. The farmer assesses the ecological impact of farming operations and seeks ways to minimize negative effects on local ecosystems, such as reducing soil erosion, preserving natural habitats, and conserving water resources.

Economic Viability: Beyond resource conservation, ZBT considers economic sustainability. The farmer evaluates the profitability of different crop choices and practices, ensuring that optimized cultivation methods result in a financially viable agricultural operation.

Continuous Learning and Adaptation: ZBT encourages a mindset of continuous learning and adaptation. The farmer remains open to new research, best practices, and emerging technologies, allowing for ongoing optimization of crop cultivation methods.

[221]

Community and Market Engagement: ZBT recognizes the importance of engaging with the community and market. The farmer seeks feedback from consumers, participates in local markets or cooperatives, and adapts crop choices to meet consumer demand while maximizing profitability.

Zero-Based Thinking applied to crop cultivation in agriculture promotes a holistic, sustainable, and adaptive approach. It encourages farmers to challenge traditional practices, embrace innovation, and optimize resource utilization to achieve higher yields, conserve natural resources, and enhance the long-term viability of their farming operations.

Retail Store Operations

Expanding on the application of Zero-Based Thinking (ZBT) in streamlining retail store operations within a retail chain:

Staffing Levels Optimization: ZBT prompts the retail chain to critically assess staffing levels at each store. This involves reevaluating employee roles, responsibilities, and scheduling to match customer traffic patterns, seasonal demands, and operational efficiency. The goal is to ensure that the right number of employees is deployed at the right times to provide excellent customer service while minimizing labor costs.

Employee Training and Development: ZBT emphasizes the importance of investing in employee training and development. Retailers ensure that staff members are well-trained in customer service, product knowledge, and operational procedures. Continuous training programs are designed to keep employees engaged and motivated.

Inventory Management Reassessment: The retail chain conducts a thorough review of its inventory management processes. ZBT encourages the adoption of advanced inventory management systems and practices, including just-in-time inventory, demand forecasting, and data analytics. This minimizes overstocking and understocking issues while optimizing inventory turnover.

Supplier Relationships: ZBT encourages retailers to reevaluate their relationships with suppliers. They consider factors like supplier reliability, cost-effectiveness, and product quality. Negotiations with suppliers may result in more favorable terms, including bulk discounts and improved delivery schedules.

Merchandising Strategies: Retailers explore new merchandising strategies based on ZBT principles. This includes revisiting store layouts, product placements, and visual merchandising techniques to enhance the customer shopping experience and boost sales.

Customer Service Excellence: ZBT places a strong focus on customer service. Retailers assess and enhance customer service practices to ensure that customers receive personalized attention, prompt assistance, and a positive shopping experience. This includes training staff in effective communication and conflict resolution.

Technology Integration: Retailers embrace technology to optimize store operations. ZBT encourages the use of point-of-sale (POS) systems, inventory management software, and customer relationship management (CRM) tools to streamline processes, gather data insights, and improve decision-making.

Loss Prevention and Security: Retail chains emphasize loss prevention and security measures. ZBT prompts the implementation of advanced security systems, surveillance technologies, and employee training to deter theft and protect store assets.

Energy Efficiency and Sustainability: ZBT recognizes the importance of environmental sustainability. Retailers assess energy consumption, waste management, and sustainable practices in their operations. Investments in energy-efficient lighting, heating, and cooling systems, as well as waste reduction initiatives, are explored.

Data-Driven Decision-Making: ZBT promotes data-driven decision-making. Retailers collect and analyze data related to customer behavior, sales trends, and operational metrics. This data informs strategic decisions, such as product assortments, pricing strategies, and promotional campaigns.

Marketing and Customer Engagement: Retail chains optimize marketing efforts based on ZBT principles. They reevaluate marketing strategies, targeting methods, and advertising channels to effectively reach and engage with their target audience, both online and offline.

Health and Safety Compliance: ZBT encourages retailers to prioritize health and safety compliance. They assess and enhance safety protocols, employee training in safety practices, and emergency response plans to ensure the well-being of customers and staff.

Zero-Based Thinking applied to retail store operations promotes a systematic and proactive approach to optimize efficiency, customer service, and profitability. It challenges established practices, embraces technology, and emphasizes the importance of continuous improvement to adapt to changing market dynamics and meet evolving customer expectations.